LIVING RIGHT SIDE UP
IN AN
UPSIDE DOWN WORLD:

ALPHABET OF DAILY LESSONS TO GIVE YOU STABILITY, HOPE AND PEACE

BY PATTI MILLER DUNHAM

If you would like to contact the author or request a speaking engagement for your group, please contact her at pattimillerdunham@me.com or through her Website at http://www. pattimillerdunham.com.

www.xulonpress.com

Lovingly dedicated to my daughter,

Natalie K. Osborne

The most loving, patient and giving person I know.

TABLE OF CONTENTS

Table of Contents

ACKNOWLEDGEMENTS

☙❧

T hank you from the bottom of my heart to my loving husband, Don, who listened to me read aloud every word written in this book. Don, your love and encouragement mean more to me than I have words to express. I love you with my whole heart, and I deeply thank God for you!

My special thanks to my editor, Carolyn Goss. Without your editing expertise, this book would not be the same. I appreciate your talents and our like-mindedness during the long process it has taken to create what God has put on my heart. You are invaluable to me, my friend, and I am so grateful God put you in my life!

To my devoted friends and family who believe in me, THANK YOU!!

NOTE FROM THE AUTHOR

☙❧

This book is a sequel to *"I Saw Heaven!": Conversations with My Brother after His Near Death Experience*. God counseled me in ways I would have never thought possible through my brother Richard. *"I Saw Heaven!"* records the God-breathed telephone conversations I had with him. Miraculously, Richard had recovered after a brief encounter with heaven as he lay in a coma, and he had shared what he had seen with us. He was a changed man. Never much of a talker, he spoke words of godly wisdom to me during eight difficult months in my life. I began spending time alone recording what Richard said to me and journaling the ways God spoke to me through him. Thus began a new chapter in my relationship with God. That relationship has grown even stronger since Richard died.

The 190-plus subjects in this book are the results of my times alone with God over the years. Each day when I woke up I knew God was waiting for me. I would just bask in His presence as the day began. As I met with God each morning, and listened, He spoke to me. Sometimes I would also read, and always I would meditate, a practice I had learned from Richard, and simple counseling from God would emerge. Early on I decided to write these words down, and I'm glad I did, because now, I find myself continually referring to these nuggets of truth. I am confident I will continue to incorporate the wisdom from God in this book into my life each day until I walk into His arms in heaven.

May you also find user-friendly truth and wisdom in the alphabetical organization of these words. Some of the entries are additional nuggets from my brother, some are directly from the Bible—but all are biblically based. God will speak to you when you make time for Him in your day. He will continue to speak to me, too, for I am continuing to learn with you. We will learn together, one day at a time.

I invite you to read *Living Right Side Up in an Upside Down World* either from cover to cover or by topics. At the end of each topic, you'll find a "Reflection" section for you to journal your interaction with what you have read and your thoughts on the accompanying words of Scripture. However you wish to read, the choice is yours!

Patti Miller Dunham, August 2013

Abundant Life

You should have life and have it more abundantly . . .

Spiritual
  Mental
    Physical
      Joyous
        Powerful
          Abundant life.
            If you follow Me you will have it.

Not all people follow Me and have this gift of an abundant life, even though I have this free gift to give to all. This is the richest gift I have to offer. Continue to accept this abundant life. Don't reject it as others do.

I delight in your enjoyment of life.

I delight in you being in My presence.

Rejoice in your gratitude for all I am to you.

Set your mind on good things above, which will enhance your enjoyment of things on earth.

I love your laughter!

ಐಜ

"I have come that they may have life, and that they may have it more abundantly." —John 10:10b NKJV

"Since, then, you have been raised with Christ, set your hearts on things above, where Christ is seated at the right hand of God. Set your minds on things above, not on earthly things. For you died, and your life is now hidden with Christ in God. When Christ, who is your life, appears, then you also will appear with him in glory." —Colossians 3:1-4

ભૂ

PRAYER

Dear God, I want this abundant life you offer me.
Guide me according to Your Will and lead me
according to Your plan for my life,
today and always.

—Amen

REFLECTION:

ACHIEVE

CC380

You can do things you've never done before with My strength. You used to hold back because of fear or no initiative. You can finish things to the end now. My strength is made perfect in your weakness. As you take one step, you will see where to take the next step. You can achieve now where before you were stifled by fear.

Take the first step. I will be with you one step at a time.

CC380

"My grace is sufficient for you, for My strength is made perfect in weakness." —2 Corinthians 12:9

"I can do all things through Christ who strengthens me." —Philippians 4:13

"He who calls you is faithful, who also will do it." —1 Thessalonians 5:24

REFLECTION:

Answers

CRSOO

There are some things that you will never have answers for. Don't fret over these things. The solutions may never be shown to you until you have left this life.

There will be the loss of dear ones, the inequality of life, the deformed and the maimed and many other puzzling things that take place. Just take one step at a time—one day at a time, and proceed on your journey, trusting Me.

Some things that are in the dark will be made clear someday. Someday you will see Me face to face.

CRSOO

"For now we see only a reflection as in a mirror; then we shall see face to face. Now I know in part; then I shall know fully, even as I am fully known."—1 Corinthians 13:12

"Do not be anxious about anything, but in everything, by prayer and petition, with thanksgiving, present your requests to God."—Philippians 4:6

REFLECTION:

ANXIETY

Nothing should seriously upset you because you have a deep, abiding faith in Me that I will take care of you.

I am your shelter from a storm. I am the power that can protect you from every temptation and defeat. Call on My divine power. Accept it and use it. Armed with My power you can face anything.

Each day, seek safety in My secret place, in communion with Me. You cannot be wholly touched or seriously harmed there. I am your refuge.

"Therefore I tell you, do not worry about your life. . . .Look at the birds of the air; they do not sow or reap or store away in barns, and yet your heavenly Father feeds them. Are you not much more valuable than they? Can any one of you by worrying add a single hour to your life?

"And why do you worry about clothes? See how the flowers of the field grow. They do not labor or spin. Yet I tell you that not even Solomon in all his splendor was dressed like

one of these. If that is how God clothes the grass of the field, which is here today and tomorrow is thrown into the fire, will he not much more clothe you. . . .But seek first his kingdom and his righteousness, and all these things will be given to you as well. Therefore do not worry about tomorrow, for tomorrow will worry about itself." —Matthew 6:25-34

REFLECTION:

ASK

CRUD

Ask Me to fill your empty vessel every day. I will fill you with My life and love. You will grow in your desire to love and serve. As you serve others I will continue to fill you up. The more you give to serve, the more you will have. You can't out give Me. Selfishness blocks you from Me and I am your source of supply. Selfishness makes you stagnant like water that has no inflow and outflow.

There is no limit as to what My power can do in a human heart. Ask for My power. My power is blocked because of indifference to it. You are going along your selfish way when you don't call out for help and ask for My power.

When you sincerely trust in Me and ask for My power, you will receive abundantly.

Pray for whatever good you may have and then leave the choice of what is good up to Me.

Ask me for anything as long as it benefits others.

CRUD

"Ask and it will be given to you; seek and you will find; knock and the door will be opened to you." —Matthew 7:7

"Every good and perfect gift is from above, coming down from the Father of the heavenly lights, who does not change like shifting shadows." —James 1:17

"Your Father knows what you need before you ask him." —Matthew 6:8

REFLECTION:

BE STILL

☙

Be still and know that I am with you.

Quiet times and communion with Me are the answers. They heighten your conscious contact with Me all day.

Sit silent before Me and I will communicate with you. I am your safe place.

I will give you direction from these times spent alone with Me.

☙

"After the earthquake came a fire, but the LORD was not in the fire. And after the fire came a gentle whisper." —1 Kings 19:12

"Be still, and know that I am God." —Psalm 46:10

REFLECTION:

BELIEVE

cs&o

I want you to believe in spiritual forces you cannot see more than material things you do see. I am real and have existed forever. You can see the results of My existence in changed lives.

Either you believe or you don't. It's your choice.

cs&o

"Now faith is confidence in what we hope for and assurance about what we do not see."
—Hebrews 11:1

REFLECTION:

BEST FRIEND

ᘓᑑ

I am your best friend. You can count on Me. As our close companionship develops you are realizing we are working to make the world a better place.

ᘓᑑ

"You are My friends if you do whatever I command you." —John 15:14

"A friend loves at all times . . ." —Proverbs 17:17

". . . there is a friend who sticks closer than a brother." —Proverbs 18:24

REFLECTION:

BLESSED

⊂ℜ℞⊃

You are blessed because you know, and are learning, the sound of My voice.

You are blessed because you are walking with Me on a daily basis.

You are blessed because you recognize My presence with you.

⊂ℜ℞⊃

"Blessed are those who have learned to acclaim you, who walk in the light of your presence, O Lord." —Psalm 89:15

REFLECTION:

BLOCKS

☙❧

I don't withhold My love from you.
I don't reject you.
I don't hold back My power from you.
I don't hide My truth from you.
I don't keep My Spirit from you.

I Am always available to you, whenever you are willing to receive Me. Check yourself for these things that might block Me: selfishness, pride, fear, worry, greed, materialism, jealousy, immorality, anger or dishonesty.

Work with Me to get rid of these blocks.

☙❧

*"You make known to me the path of life; you will fill me with joy in your presence, with eternal pleasures at your right hand." —*Psalm 7:4, 8

REFLECTION:

CALMNESS

ᘓ৪০

Try to stay calm no matter what happens. The day might bring disturbances and others' emotions might flare up, but keep your emotions calm because I am with you and you can call on My strength.

Be still and commune with Me.

The eternal life I have for you is calmness. When you enter into calmness you are living your eternal life. Calmness is based on complete trust in Me. Nothing in this world can separate you from My love.

Wear the world like a loose garment.

Keep calm at the center of your being.

Staying calm is so important. "Be still and know that I am God." Trusting Me can keep you calm. Seek things that give you calmness.

Life will put you in the midst of storms. Learn the lessons of trust and calm in these storms. Whatever the day may bring, be grateful, humble, calm, and loving to all people.

Leave each person better for having met you. Your attitude should be a calm, loving desire to help others as you trust in Me.

You have the answer to fear and personal problems, which is faith in My goodness and love.

ᏣᎬᎤ

"Be still and know that I am God."
—Psalm 46:10

"Do not let your hearts be troubled. You believe in God; believe also in me."
—John 14:27

"Do not be anxious about anything, but in every situation, by prayer and petition, with thanksgiving, present your requests to God. [7] And the peace of God, which transcends all understanding, will guard your hearts and your minds in Christ Jesus."—Philippians 4:6-7

REFLECTION:

CHALLENGES

❧

Don't try to do things without My help. That's why you make a mess of things. You can do nothing of any value without My help.

I am here to help you, to bless you, and to accompany you.

Through challenges you are being transformed from character to character. My grace is changing you.

Even though you don't feel it, you are on the glorious upward way.

❧

"Though I walk in the midst of trouble, you preserve my life. You stretch out your hand against the anger of my foes; with your right hand you save me." —Psalm 138:7

"We are hard pressed on every side, but not crushed; perplexed, but not in despair; persecuted, but not abandoned; struck down, but not destroyed." —2 Corinthians 4:8-9

"Let us then approach God's throne of grace with confidence, so that we may receive

mercy and find grace to help us in our time of need." —Hebrews 4:16

REFLECTION:

CHANGE

⊂⨯⨝⊃

Ask Me to give you strength to change daily. When you ask Me to change you, you must fully trust Me. Don't resist and your life will continue to go forward in peace.

My mercy for you is great. My grace is sufficient to give you peace and hope. Change is possible with Me.

You can be sure that people's lives can change. Changes in a person's life are natural to Me. Miracles happen in a person's life because they accept My grace and mercy. People surrender to My grace because they long for something better and have a real desire for change.

Never give up praying for anyone.

A spiritual experience brings about a personality change. Surrendering and realizing that things are hopeless without Me is a spiritual experience. In most cases the change will be gradual.

⊂⨯⨝⊃

"But he said to me, 'My grace is sufficient for you, for my power is made perfect in weakness.' Therefore I will boast all the more gladly about my weaknesses, so that Christ's power may rest on me." —2 Corinthians 12:9

REFLECTION:

CHARACTER

൭൮

Character is developed by spending time with Me and the daily discipline of duties accomplished.

Prayer and meditation are key components because you will receive guidance. Rest and wait patiently for My guidance.

Daily duties are character building because I have made you in My image and I am a Creator and Finisher. I'm with you during your daily duties.

൭൮

"So whether you eat or drink or whatever you do, do it all for the glory of God." —1 Corinthians 10:12

REFLECTION:

CHILDLIKE

☙❧

No matter your age, I want you to be childlike in these things:

- Trust Me.
- Enjoy life and laugh often.
- Lack criticism.
- Have a desire to share.
- Stay humble.
- Be forgiving.
- Be loving.

With these attributes you will be the greatest in the kingdom of heaven.

☙❧

". . . If it is to encourage, then give encouragement; if it is giving, then give generously; if it is to lead, do it diligently; if it is to show mercy, do it cheerfully." —Romans 12:8

" . . . Whoever takes the lowly position of this child is the greatest in the kingdom of heaven." —Matthew 18:4

REFLECTION:

CHOICES

CREC

You have choices to make between the physical view or the spiritual view of life. The physical view will be guided by coveting wealth, envy, pride, greed, dishonesty, and selfishness. The spiritual view will be guided by peace, faith, honesty, unselfishness, hope, love, and a desire to serve others.

You have a choice. You can't choose both. When you make the right choice you are going forward to success and I am rejoicing with you in heaven.

Every minute is filled with choices—choices to draw you away from Me or to draw you closer to Me.

Choosing life means choosing Me.

CREC

"This day I call the heavens and the earth as witnesses against you that I have set before you life and death, blessings and curses. Now choose life, so that you and your children may live."—Deuteronomy 30:19

REFLECTION:

CHOICES II

രൂ

You have a choice to live your own way or My way.

We are conditioning your conscious mind daily so your unconscious mind will have thoughts less and less about making wrong choices. You might dream you have made wrong choices right now, but those dreams will become less frequent because of spending quality communion with Me on a daily basis.

You are now spiritually guided when you make choices because you've given Me your life and your will today. I will guide you into truth. My plans for you are good and My Will will be done.

When faced with a choice, ask yourself: Will this choice bring me closer to God?

Choose the good and you will feel My power supporting you. Your choice of good will take you forward to true success and victory. Choose to live today with faith, hope, and love. You can choose your attitude.

Every time you have chosen character over convenience, faithfulness over ease, or honestly over deceit, you have brought honor to Me.

You have been given free will to choose. You can choose the path with Me, which is good. You can choose the path without Me, which is bad.

Choosing the right path will take you to eternal life that is full of love, peace, and joy unspeakable.

CB∞

But if serving the Lord *seems undesirable to you, then choose for yourselves this day whom you will serve, whether the gods your ancestors served beyond the Euphrates, or the gods of the Amorites, in whose land you are living. But as for me and my household, we will serve the* Lord. —Joshua 24:15

REFLECTION:

CHOSEN

☙

I picked you out for Myself before the foundations of
the world.
I knew you when you were being formed in your
mother's womb.
I've watched you grow. I've never left you. I know all
about you and love you.
My thoughts of you number more than the grains of sand.
I have your picture indelibly printed on the palm of each
of My hands.
You are in My thoughts constantly.
I never forget you.
You are the apple of My eye.

☙

*"For he chose us in him before the creation
of the world to be holy and blameless in his
sight."* —Ephesians 1:4

*"Be strong and courageous. Do not be afraid
or terrified because of them, for the LORD
your God goes with you; he will never leave
you nor forsake you."* —Deuteronomy 31:6

"Keep your lives free from the love of money and be content with what you have, because God has said, 'Never will I leave you; never will I forsake you.'" —Hebrews 13:5

"In a desert land he found him [Jacob], in a barren and howling waste. He shielded him and cared for him; he guarded him as the apple of his eye." —Deuteronomy 32:10

"My frame was not hidden from you when I was made in the secret place, when I was woven together in the depths of the earth. Your eyes saw my unformed body; all the days ordained for me were written in your book before one of them came to be. How precious to me are your thoughts, God! How vast is the sum of them! Were I to count them, they would outnumber the grains of sand—when I awake, I am still with you." —Psalm 139:15-18

"You did not choose me, but I chose you and appointed you so that you might go and bear fruit—fruit that will last—and so that whatever you ask in my name the Father will give you." —John 15:16

REFLECTION:

COME TO ME

⊂3⊃

Come to Me for the things to help you live:
For the solution to every problem,
For the overcoming of every temptation,
For the calming of every fear,
For all your spiritual, physical, and mental needs.
Most of all, come to Me for the strength you need to live with peace of mind and the power to be useful and effective.

Come to Me with your emotions over life's realities. Don't go to any substance or crutch. Don't try to cover or drown your emotions.

Talk to Me. When you have mental conflicts, come to Me. You will never experience anything I didn't. I love you.

⊂3⊃

"For we do not have a high priest who is unable to empathize with our weaknesses, but we have one who has been tempted in every way, just as we are—yet he did not sin. Let us then approach God's throne of grace with confidence, so that we may receive mercy and find grace to help us in our time of need." —Hebrews 4:15-16

"Come to me, all you who are weary and burdened, and I will give you rest."
—Matthew 11:28

REFLECTION:

COMFORT

తళ

I am your source of comfort. I will comfort you in every trouble, calamity, or affliction.

తళ

"Praise be to the God and Father of our Lord Jesus Christ, the Father of compassion and the God of all comfort. . ." —2 Corinthians 1:3

"I will turn their mourning into gladness; I will give them comfort and joy instead of sorrow." —Jeremiah 31:13

"As a mother comforts her child, so will I comfort you; and you will be comforted over Jerusalem." —Isaiah 66:13

"Record my misery; list my tears on your scroll—are they not in your record? Then my enemies will turn back when I call for help. By this I will know that God is for me. In God, whose word I praise, in the LORD, whose word I praise—in God I trust and am not afraid. What can man do to me? —Psalm 56:13

REFLECTION:

COMPASSION

☾⊰✿⊱☽

When you are moved with compassion, not pity, go and do what you are capable of doing for that person. You have been tempted like they were. You have made wrong choices like they have. You have had circumstances happen beyond your control as they have.

I am compassion.

Bind up their wounds.

☾⊰✿⊱☽

The Spirit of the Sovereign Lord is on me, because the Lord has anointed me to proclaim good news to the poor. He has sent me to bind up the brokenhearted, to proclaim freedom for the captives and release from darkness for the prisoners, to proclaim the year of the Lord's favor and the day of vengeance of our God, to comfort all who mourn, and provide for those who grieve in Zion— to bestow on them a crown of beauty instead of ashes, the oil of joy instead of mourning, and a garment of praise instead of a spirit of despair. They will be called oaks of righteousness, a planting of the Lord for the display of his splendor.—Isaiah 61:1-3

REFLECTION:

CONFIDENCE

⋯

Confidence and faith are the same things.

- You can have confidence in My grace, and you will be able to face whatever comes.
- You can have confidence in My love, and this will give you peace.
- You can have confidence that I will take care of you, and this will give you rest.
- You can rest in My presence until My power for life flows through you.

Be still, and My small voice will come to you in the stillness.

⋯

"But he said to me, 'My grace is sufficient for you, for my power is made perfect in weakness.' Therefore I will boast all the more gladly about my weaknesses, so that Christ's power may rest on me." —2 Corinthians 12:9

"And my God will meet all your needs according to the riches of his glory in Christ Jesus." — Philippians 4:19

"I can do all this through him who gives me strength." — Philippians 4:13

REFLECTION:

CONFLICTS

෴

Ask God's blessings on those you are in conflict with. Love them into My hands.

Don't live with conflicts with yourself.

You will have peace when these three things line up:
What you think
What you say
What you do

Let Me guide you in all human relationships. Rely on My power to deal with people. I will give you wisdom to put things right.

෴

"Bless those who curse you, pray for those who mistreat you. . ." —Luke 6:28

REFLECTION:

Confusion

❧

I am not a God of confusion and disorder. I am a God of peace and order.

You have taken control when you are confused. Confusion causes fear and panic.

Come back to Me. Give each thing to Me. Wait for My answer.

Sometimes you simply need to do what's in front of you that has to be done.

Do things decently and in order, one thing at a time.

❧

"For God is not the author of confusion but of peace . . ." — 1 Corinthians 14:33

"Let all things be done decently and in order." — 1 Corinthians 14:40 NKJV

REFLECTION:

CONTROL

෴

You are learning you can't control people, places, or things. You don't have that power. You can't produce change in the lives of others. Change will come only if they see Me through you. This produces a spiritual power that changes lives.

Remember this: You are not running the world.

Pray and relax.

෴

Trust in the LORD with all your heart and lean not on your own understanding; in all your ways submit to him, and he will make your paths straight. Do not be wise in your own eyes; fear the LORD and shun evil. This will bring health to your body and nourishment to your bones. —Proverbs 3:5-8

REFLECTION:

CRITICISM FROM OTHERS

ᚙᚙ

First of all, remember what I have taught you. It does not matter what others think about you, and you can't do anything about their thoughts. All that matters is what *you think about them.*

I am your only judge. Try never to judge.

Don't fear displeasing others, because then you will become in bondage to them. Refocus your thoughts on Me and start saying My name. Spend time alone with Me.

Don't fall back into your old pattern of wondering how you appear to others and what you think they are thinking of you, and then trying to please them by reacting to what you think they are thinking. Don't go there!

I convict you with My love, mercy, and grace. I am your Lord and no other will be Lord again of your life.

Don't "should" on yourself. That keeps you from going forward.

If you've made a mistake, own up to it and ask for forgiveness.

Try never to judge because the human mind is so complex that only I know it. Each mind is different from every other mind because it's been affected by different life experiences, circumstances, and sufferings.

Leave it to Me to teach you understanding.

No weapon that is formed against thee shall prosper; and every tongue that shall rise against thee in judgment thou shalt condemn. This is the heritage of the servants of the LORD, and their righteousness is of me, saith the LORD. —Isaiah 54:17 KJV

When the LORD takes pleasure in anyone's way, he causes their enemies to make peace with them.—*Proverbs 16:7*

CustⳠ

REFLECTION:

CRITICIZE

ᘓᆓᘑ

Become less critical of others—because when you are running down others, you are unconsciously trying to build yourself up.

Don't envy or hate. Don't think you are better than others. Don't look for faults in others so you can tear them down. You cannot ever make other people better by criticizing them.

A better way is to look for the good in others. Make your job to try to bring out the good. Do not criticize the bad. Encourage others' good points and ignore their bad points. People are never changed by criticism.

Don't criticize others, period! When you see a toothpick in someone else's eye you usually have a log in your own eye. It's not your place to criticize others, period.

You are not running the world. Wear this world as a loose garment and keep your focus on Me.

ᘓᆓᘑ

"How can you say to your brother, 'Let me take the speck out of your eye,' when all the time there is a plank in your own eye? You hypocrite, first take the plank out of your own eye, and then you will see clearly

to remove the speck from your brother's eye." —Matthew 7:1-5

REFLECTION:

CRY OUT

୦୫୫୦

Your cry out to Me never goes unheard. I always hear you and I will always answer.

Trust Me to answer the way I see fit.

Pray that you will be content with whatever form the answer will be.

Your cry, a trusting cry, pierces through the darkness and reaches My ear.

୦୫୫୦

"Let us then approach God's throne of grace with confidence, so that we may receive mercy and find grace to help us in our time of need." —Hebrews 4:16

"This poor man called, and the LORD heard him; he saved him out of all his troubles." — Psalm 34:6

"In my distress I called to the LORD; I cried to my God for help. From his temple he heard my voice; my cry came before him, into his ears." —Psalm 18:6

REFLECTION:

DAILY

Your first step daily is to give your life and your will to Me. This is your offering. Lay yourself on the altar, ready for Me to do what's best for you. When you trust Me you will know I will do what is best for you.

Secondly, be confident that what I do for you will be for the best. Be confident that I am powerful enough to do anything I will and that no miracle in a human life is possible without Me. Then leave the future to Me.

Thirdly, live in the present. Forget the past as much as possible, except to learn from it or make restitution if need be. Go on in faith. Each step will get lighter and clearer.

I have no reproach for anyone I have healed. Go forward whole and free.

Enjoy all the good things and the beauty of life, but at the same time depend totally on Me.

"Jesus straightened up and asked her, 'Woman, where are they? Has no one condemned you?' 'No one, sir,' she said. 'Then neither do I condemn you,' Jesus declared. 'Go now and leave your life of sin.'" — John 8:10-12

"So do not worry or be anxious about tomorrow, for tomorrow will have worries and anxieties of its own. Sufficient for each day is its own trouble." — Matthew 6:34 AMP

REFLECTION:

DECISION

☙❧

I will guide you to the right decisions if you will pray about them. Pray to be shown the right way. I guide you through reading My Word, the Bible. I guide you through listening. I guide you through right and wrong. Always choose right. I counsel you through your conscience.

☙❧

"Your word is a lamp for my feet, a light on my path." —Psalm 119:105

"I will instruct you and teach you in the way you should go; I will counsel you with my loving eye on you." —Psalm 32:8

"For this God is our God forever and ever; He will be our guide [even] until death." — Psalm 48:14 AMP

"But when He, the Spirit of Truth (the Truth-giving Spirit) comes, He will guide you into all the Truth (the whole, full Truth). For He will not speak His own message [on His own authority]; but He will tell whatever

He hears [from the Father; He will give the message that has been given to Him], and He will announce and declare to you the things that are to come [that will happen in the future.]" —John 16:13 AMP

REFLECTION:

DESPAIR

❧

Thankfulness is the remedy to despair. Give Me your gift of a thankful heart. Look for reasons to be thankful. Make a gratitude list.

I am thankful:

- That I am God's child.
- That I know you, Jesus.
- That I am healthy.
- That I have such a wonderful job.
- For my family and friends.
- For my home and my car.
- For air to breathe.
- That I can hear and see.

❧

"Though the fig tree does not bud and there are no grapes on the vines, though the olive crop fails and the fields produce no food, though there are no sheep in the pen and no cattle in the stalls, yet I will rejoice in the LORD, I will be joyful in God my Savior." —Habakkuk 3:17-18

"I have told you these things, so that in me you may have peace. In this world you will

have trouble. But take heart! I have overcome
the world." — John 16:33

"So do not throw away your confidence;
it will be richly rewarded. You need to
persevere so that when you have done the
will of God, you will receive what he has
promised." —Hebrews 10:35-36

"No temptation has overtaken you except
such as is common to man; but God is
faithful, who will not allow you to be tempted
beyond what you are able, but with the temptation will also make the way of escape, that
you may be able to bear it." —1 Corinthians
10:13 NKJV

". . . being confident of this very thing, that
He who has begun a good work in you will
complete it until the day of Jesus Christ. . ."
—Philippians 1:6 NKJV

REFLECTION:

DESTINY

⁂

I have brought you through the ups and downs of life to a place of real usefulness in this world. I have let you live for this.

This is your opportunity and your destiny.

You are worth something.

Let your light shine.

⁂

"For you created my inmost being; you knit me together in my mother's womb. I praise you because I am fearfully and wonderfully made; our works are wonderful, I know that full well. My frame was not hidden from you when I was made in the secret place, when I was woven together in the depths of the earth. Your eyes saw my unformed body; all the days ordained for me were written in your book before one of them came to be. How precious to me are your thoughts, God! How vast is the sum of them! Were I to count them, they would outnumber the grains of sand— when I awake, I am still with you."
—Psalm 139:13-18

"He lifted me out of the slimy pit, out of the mud and mire; he set my feet on a rock and gave me a firm place to stand. He put a new song in my mouth, a hymn of praise to our God. Many will see and fear the LORD and put their trust in him." —Psalm 40:2-3 AMP

"For I know the plans I have for you," declares the LORD, *"plans to prosper you and not to harm you, plans to give you hope and a future."* —Jeremiah 29:11

REFLECTION:

DEVIL

❧

The Devil is real. He is as real as I am, but he has no personal interest in you. He is only out to hurt Me because I gave my life for you. One way to do that is to hurt the ones I love, and that means you.

You can stop him in his tracks. First, remember this: Submit to Me, resist him, and he has to flee.

He is only a prideful, fallen angel. He isn't all-knowing and all-powerful. Yet, he can cause trouble.

Take a stand. Don't give the Devil free rent in your head.

I defeated the Devil when I died on the cross and rose again.

Stick close to Me. Keep your eyes on Me. Use My name and Who I am to resist him.

❧

"Submit yourselves, then, to God. Resist the devil, and he will flee from you." —James 4:7

"You, dear children, are from God and have overcome them, because the one who is in you is greater than the one who is in the world." —1 John 4:3-4

"Therefore put on the full armor of God, so that when the day of evil comes, you may be able to stand your ground, and after you have done everything, to stand." —Ephesians 6:13

"You are of God, little children, and have overcome them, because He who is in you is greater than he who is in the world." —1 John 4:4 NKJV

REFLECTION:

DIFFICULTIES

CREO

You will have difficulties or troubles in life, but here is what I want you to do.

- Stay calm and unshaken.
- Keep your faith.
- Be courageous.

You can do these things by resting and leaning on Me. Remember that I am here for you. As you keep your eyes on Me, I will give you peace in the midst of the storm. Lean into Me. Remember, I have overcome the world. Don't be afraid.

CREO

"I have told you these things, so that in me you may have peace. In this world you will have trouble. But take heart! I have overcome the world." —John 16:33

"For our light and momentary troubles are achieving for us an eternal glory that far outweighs them all." —2 Corinthians 4:17

CREO

You can have peace in the midst of difficulties by faithfully trusting and accepting My will, even when you are surrounded by troubles.

Difficulties and troubles test your strength and build your character.

Don't fear difficult struggles in life, because I know what you can bear. Look to the future with confidence and know I will be with you and give you what it takes to overcome.

ೞ৪০

No temptation has overtaken you except what is common to mankind. And God is faithful; he will not let you be tempted beyond what you can bear. But when you are tempted, he will also provide a way out so that you can endure it. — 1 Corinthians 10:13

REFLECTION:

DIRECTION

ᚙ

I will give you direction. Listen. Meditate. Your problems come when you don't follow it.

ᚙ

"I will instruct you and teach you in the way you should go; I will counsel you with my loving eye on you." —Psalm 32:8

"Commit your works to the LORD, and your thoughts will be established." —Proverbs 16:3 NKJV

"The LORD makes firm the steps of the one who delights in him." —Psalm 37:23

"If any of you lacks wisdom, you should ask God, who gives generously to all without finding fault, and it will be given to you." —James 1:5

REFLECTION:

DISCIPLINE

CR&O

You have discovered that discipline in your life gives you the best life. Every champion has learned discipline. The higher you rise on the scale of responsibility, the greater is the necessity of discipline in your life. This is one of My character traits and you are becoming more and more like Me.

CR&O

"For lack of discipline they will die, led astray by their own great folly." —Proverbs 55:23

REFLECTION:

DISHARMONY

⊂ॐ⊃

My grace will guide you through disharmony and disorder, one day at a time. Put the situation in My hands along with the confusion and the people.

I will guide you through and I can be your shield. Nothing can have the power to spoil your inward peace. With Me as your shield, you can attain this inward peace quickly in your surroundings, as well as in your heart. Don't resent the person who troubles you. Instead, give them to Me and go on about your business.

When you have disharmony with others, say of the other person, "God bless her (or him)." Be willing for showers of blessings to fall on them. Let Me do the blessing and leave the discipline and outcome to Me. Occupy yourself with what I've given you to do.

⊂ॐ⊃

"For God is not the author of confusion but of peace, as in all the churches of the saints."
—1 Corinthians 14:33

" . . . My God is my rock, in whom I take refuge, my shield and the horn of my salvation. He is my stronghold, my refuge and my

savior—from violent people you save me.—2 Samuel 22:3

*"But you, LORD, are a shield around me, my glory, the One who lifts my head high."—*Psalm 3:3

*"The LORD is my strength and my shield; my heart trusts in him, and he helps me. My heart leaps for joy, and with my song I praise him."—*Psalm 28:7

*"For the LORD GOD is a sun and shield; the LORD bestows favor and honor; no good thing does he withhold from those whose walk is blameless."—*Psalm 84:11

*"He will cover you with his feathers, and under his wings you will find refuge; his faithfulness will be your shield and rampart."—*Psalm 91:4

*"...bless those who curse you, pray for those who mistreat you."—*Luke 6:28

*" . . . In God I trust and am not afraid. What can man do to me?"—*Psalm 56:11

"Am I now trying to win the approval of human beings, or of God? Or am I trying to please people? If I were still trying to please people, I would not be a servant of Christ."
—Galatians 1:10

"So we say with confidence, 'The Lord is my helper; I will not be afraid. What can mere mortals do to me?'" —*Hebrews 13:6*

REFLECTION:

DISORDER

૭૪૦

I made the ordered world out of chaos and set each planet on its course. I made each plant to know its season and gave each animal its instincts. If I can do this, I can bring order out of your private chaos if you will let Me.

I am watching over you to care for and to bless you. I am leading you . . .

out of darkness into light

out of unrest into rest

out of disorder into order

and out of faults and failure into success.

You belong to Me. Your affairs are My affairs. I can order them if you are willing. I am a God of order.

૭૪૦

"Guard your steps when you go to the house of God. Go near to listen rather than to offer the sacrifice of fools, who do not know that they do wrong." —Ecclesiastes 5:1

"These have come so that the proven genuineness of your faith—of greater worth than gold, which perishes even though refined by

fire—may result in praise, glory and honor when Jesus Christ is revealed." —1 Peter 4:7

REFLECTION:

DIVIDING WALLS

CRITICAL

Your faith and My power can accomplish much. Walls that divide you from another human being can fall by your faith and My power.

Strengthen your faith day by day and rely more on My power.

CRITICAL

"He who deals wisely and heeds [God's] word and counsel shall find good, and whoever leans on, trusts in, and is confident in the Lord—happy, blessed, and fortunate is he." —Proverbs 16:19-20 AMP

"Yet to all who did receive him, to those who believed in his name, he gave the right to become children of God." —John 1:12

". . . so that your faith might not rest on human wisdom, but on God's power." —1 Corinthians 2:5

REFLECTION:

DOING "TOMORROW" THINKING

CREO

Don't bring into your thoughts today what you might do "tomorrow," rehearsing what you will do or say. When you do that, you are in control. Being self-sufficient is not trusting Me.

Trust Me enough to let things happen without striving and manipulating. I will work everything together for your good and My glory.

CREO

"For I know the plans I have for you," declares the LORD, "plans to prosper you and not to harm you, plans to give you hope and a future." —Jeremiah 29:11

"But seek (aim at and strive after) first of all His kingdom and His righteousness (His way of doing and being right), and then all these things taken together will be given you besides. So do not worry or be anxious about tomorrow, for tomorrow will have worries and anxieties of its own. Sufficient for each day is its own trouble." —Matthew 6:33-34 AMP

REFLECTION:

DOUBT

⚭

Don't doubt My power and take things in your own hands. When you are doubting My goodness, you are in control again. This doubt can spoil life and you won't live to your full potential. You won't stand tall and face life with an affirmative attitude. Don't lower yourself by allowing doubt to bring you down. Lift your head high and keep your eyes of faith on Me. I love you and will lead you in the right paths. Keep cultivating your desire to do the right thing. That is where your blessings are.

⚭

"But when you ask, you must believe and not doubt, because the one who doubts is like a wave of the sea, blown and tossed by the wind." —James 1:6

"Then he said to Thomas, 'Put your finger here; see my hands. Reach out your hand and put it into my side. Stop doubting and believe.'" —John 20:27

" . . . he refreshes my soul. He guides me along the right paths or his name's sake."
—Psalm 23:3

REFLECTION:

DOWN ON YOURSELF

රිෂ්ව

Don't get down on yourself.

Don't look at your past failures and mistakes. Doing that keeps you from going forward.

You've asked Me to forgive you for all those things and I have forgotten them and put them as far as the East is from the West. Holding things over your own head after you have been forgiven is prideful and self-destructive.

Have you ceased being mentally at war with yourself? You've asked Me to forgive you and I have. I don't remember the transgression anymore. Now you need to forgive yourself, and do it quickly.

Stay on course.

Keep your thoughts on Me.

Keep your faith.

Keep your focus on doing right.

Keep your focus on loving Me and loving others.

And, keep your focus on loving yourself.

Don't dwell on mistakes, faults and failures of the past. Be done with shame, remorse, and contempt for yourself. With My help, develop a new self-respect for yourself. Unless you respect yourself, others will not respect you.

In running your race, you stumbled and fell. Pick yourself up. Brush yourself off and begin again. Don't get caught up in examining where you fell and why you fell. This keeps you from going forward.

Don't look back.

Keep picking yourself up each day and go forward.

I'm with you.

⋘⋙

"As a prisoner for the Lord, then, I urge you to live a life worthy of the calling you have received." —Ephesians 4:1

"Submit to God and be at peace with him; in this way prosperity will come to you." —Job 22:21

". . . looking for the blessed hope and glorious appearing of our great God and Savior Jesus Christ. . ." —Titus 2:13

REFLECTION:

DOWN ON YOURSELF II

൦ൠ

Sometimes you have this nagging feeling that you've done something wrong. Run to Me and say My name over and over. Many times you've done nothing wrong—you are just tired. I'm not against you.

I can make a difference in the way you face life. Beating yourself up is not My way. Get out of the ring and refuse to beat yourself up. My eye is on the sparrow and I'm also watching and loving you, too.

Rebuke these thoughts in My name. Don't give them free rent in your head. You've seen Me. You know Me. What does anything else matter?

Do you feel like you've disappointed someone? Did you do anything wrong? I'm the only one you need to receive true acceptance from. Has people pleasing kicked in? That goes back to perfectionism. You'll never be perfect.

Turn your back on pride.

Repent of wanting to please a person.

My acceptance is all you need. Remember, it doesn't matter what others think of you. All that matters is what you think of them.

൦ൠ

"The LORD is with me; I will not be afraid. What can mere mortals do to me?" — Psalm 118:6

"What, then, shall we say in response to these things? If God is for us, who can be against us?" — Romans 8:31

"Look at the birds of the air; they do not sow or reap or store away in barns, and yet your heavenly Father feeds them. Are you not much more valuable than they?" — Matt 6:26

REFLECTION:

EFFECTIVENESS

⋈

Your effectiveness depends on My strength. Are you held back by self-consciousness or fear? Self-consciousness is a form of pride. It is a fear that something might happen to you.

Look to Me for the true power to be effective.
See no other wholly dependable supply of strength.
That's the secret of a truly effective life.

Seek God's Will in your life. Seek to know that your will conforms to My Will. That's when your life will be truly effective. Failure comes from depending too much on your own strength.

⋈

"I can do all things through Christ who strengthens me." —Philippians 4:13

REFLECTION:

EMOTIONAL UPSET

Cଃଃଠ

Don't let emotional upsets weaken your faith. Your faith is your lifeline. On one end is your soul and spirit. I am on the other end. Faith keeps the lifeline strong.

Trust in Me and don't be afraid. Look to Me for help and trust Me for aid when you are emotionally upset.

Keep a strong hold onto your lifeline of faith.

Faith in Me stabilizes your emotions. Keep a proper perspective on life, and remember that most things you are tempted to fear never happen. A problem may seem big at the moment, but remember, "This, too, shall pass." They don't stick around.

Continually give problems to Me and don't take them back. Leave the outcome to me by praying, "Thy Will be done."

You cannot afford to lose your lifeline when you are tempted to make wrong choices. Anything that causes you to lose your peace is not worth it. You are tempted to say or do the wrong thing when you are emotionally upset.

Don't get steamed up over anything.
Don't let your emotions rule your actions.

Cଃଃଠ

"Peace I leave with you; my peace I give you. I do not give to you as the world gives. Do not let your hearts be troubled and do not be afraid." —John 14:27

"Do not let your hearts be troubled. You believe in God; believe also in me." —John 14:1

"I have told you these things, so that in me you may have peace. In this world you will have trouble. But take heart! I have overcome the world." —John 16:33

"You will keep in perfect peace those whose minds are steadfast, because they trust in you." —Isaiah 26:3

REFLECTION:

Encouragement

You can't do anything about what happens *to* you,
But you can do something about what happens *in* you.
It's not what happens to you but how you take it
that matters.

You have My Holy Spirit in you to help you deal with anything. He is your guide, your Counselor, your Comforter, your Friend, and your Helper.

Don't ask "why?" Ask "how?" How am I dealing with this?

Ask for My strength. When you are weak, I am strong. I'm on your side. If your heart is right, your world will be right.

Seek to right what is inside you. As you improve yourself *inwardly*, your *outward* will improve.

Seek Me, inquire of Me, and crave My strength.
I am an Encourager, and you can be the same to others.
I am here and you can depend on Me.
The hard times you are facing will end.
I hear your cry and I am answering your prayers.

"And I will ask the Father, and He will give you another Comforter (Counselor, Helper,

Intercessor, Advocate, Strengthener, and Standby), that He may remain with you forever . . ." —John 14:16 7:14 AMP

"Seek, inquire of and for the LORD, and crave Him and His strength (His might and inflexibility to temptation); seek and require His face and His presence [continually] evermore." —Psalm 105:4 AMP

". . . that is, that you and I may be mutually encouraged by each other's faith." —Romans 1:12

"If My people, who are called by My name, shall humble themselves, pray, seek, crave, and require of necessity My face and turn from their wicked ways, then will I hear from heaven, forgive their sin, and heal their land." —2 Chronicles 7:14 AMP

REFLECTION:

ENVY

❦

You have gotten rid of the poison of envy. Wanting what others have causes tremendous discontent in your soul. You are putting your efforts and thoughts toward Me and this brings contentment. The right things will come your way because of this new way of living.

❦

"Trust in the LORD with all your heart and lean not on your own understanding; in all your ways submit to him, and he will make your paths straight."
—Proverbs 3:5-6

"A heart at peace gives life to the body, but envy rots the bones." —Proverbs 14:30 NIV

"Love is patient, love is kind. It does not envy, it does not boast, it is not proud." —1 Corinthians 13:4

REFLECTION:

Eternal Life

❦

Learning to know Me better is drawing you to eternal life. Eternal life with Me is real. Your life on earth is preparation for life to come in heaven.

I have given you abundant eternal life. This life doesn't begin when you enter heaven. It is in the here and now because "the kingdom of God is within you."

Live your life each day as though it were your last.

❦

"Now this is eternal life: that they know you, the only true God, and Jesus Christ, whom you have sent." —John 17:3

"For God so loved the world that he gave his one and only Son, that whoever believes in him shall not perish but have eternal life." —John 3:16

". . . nor will people say, 'Here it is,' or 'There it is,' because the kingdom of God is in your midst." —Luke 17:21

REFLECTION:

EXPECTATIONS

CЗ800

Expectations are planned disappointments.

Don't expect to have what you are not prepared for.

Want My Will above all things.

Help others to find My Will for them.

There is a major difference between hope and expectations. There can be a demanding aspect to expectations. Hope suggests confidence and assurance that I know best. You can have hope because of My promises.

Remember, you cannot control people, places or things. You don't have that power. Turn your life and will over to Me and don't have expectations. Give others to Me in the same way.

CЗ800

*"For I know the plans I have for you,"
declares the* LORD, *"plans to prosper you and
not to harm you, plans to give you hope and a
future."*—Jeremiah 29:11

REFLECTION:

FAILURE

૭૩૮૦

Your life will have setbacks, mistakes, and failures, but you are not a failure. You are going forward because you have learned to put Me first.

You've learned to come to Me—and that is success.

You've learned to go forward with faith after coming to Me. You have hope for the future because it will be good. You are developing and growing through every experience, which will be used for good in this world.

You are not a failure and as you go forward, it will be good. Failure is when you attempt to live without Me.

૭૩૮૦

"The LORD makes firm the steps of the one who delights in him; though he may stumble, he will not fall, for the Lord upholds him with his hand." —Psalm 37: 23-24

"Let us not become weary in doing good, for at the proper time we will reap a harvest if we do not give up." —Galatians 6:9

REFLECTION:

FAITH

᙭᙭

To see Me through your eyes of faith is to cause My power to manifest.

I cannot do My work because of people's unbelief. Because of unbelief I do not manifest My power. In response to your faith I work miracles in your personality.

Believing in My never-failing power will change you. You can only see Me through the eyes of faith, but when you do, great changes happen in your way of living.

Faith in Me can help you overcome loneliness, fear,
and anxiety.
Faith can help you get along with other people.
Faith can make it possible for you to rise above pain,
sorrow, and despondency.
Faith can help you overcome desires for things that destroy.
Faith is not seeing but believing. My grace is available to
you because of your faith.
Faith is an act of your mind and will.
Renew it every morning during our quiet time together.

᙭᙭

"For it is by grace you have been saved, through faith—and this is not from yourselves, it is the gift of God." —Ephesians 2:8

REFLECTION:

FAITH II

CℬℰO

You know there is more to life than meets the eye. I have done things no human being can do.

Pray for faith as a thirsty person would pray for water in the desert. Feel sure that I will never fail you. Feel as sure of this promise to you as you are of the air you breathe. Pray that your faith would increase. Realize that I have everything you need.

Faith is knowing that God will never fail you.
Faith isn't a sign of weakness. It is a sign of strength.
For the peaceful life you desire, absolute faith and trust in
Me is the key.

CℬℰO

*"As the deer pants for streams of water, so my
soul pants for you, my God." —Psalm 42:1*

REFLECTION:

Faith III

৩৪০

You are finding that faith makes sense. I am holding the universe that I created together and there is order, meaning, and purpose to it. Faith is giving you meaning and purpose. The reward it gives you is peace.

The way of faith is the way of life. Many are lost without it. You have found the way.

Let faith in Me be the controlling factor in your life. Without faith your life becomes scattered, meaningless, and disorganized.

When you live by faith and not by sight you will see My glory. You will see Me in everything throughout your day.

Faith is part of your make up. It is part of you.
Be real with Me. I am real.

Work at strengthening your faith. Pray for faith every day, for faith is a gift. It is necessary for you to live the Christian life. With faith, you'll find that My power becomes available to you.

৩৪০

"Now faith is confidence in what we hope for and assurance about what we do not see."—Hebrews 11:1a

REFLECTION:

FEAR

ை80ை

As faith replaces fear, you are maturing. You've learned you cannot have fear and faith at the same time. You are seeing the results of this new way of living through your family and other relationships and through parts of your life.

You have gained peace, contentment, hope, faith, and love.

You have lost paralyzing fear, dread, and worry.

Don't ever let fear motivate you to make decisions.

Fear is disloyalty to Me.
Avoid fear like a plague.

Fear starts chipping away from our strong secure relationship. Have such trust in Me that fear doesn't have a chance.

Don't fear evil. Place yourself under My protection, My grace, and My name.

ை80ை

"For I am persuaded that neither death nor life, nor angels nor principalities nor powers, nor things present nor things to come, nor height nor depth, nor any other created thing, shall be able to separate us from the love

of God which is in Christ Jesus our Lord.”
—Romans 8:38-39 NKJV

“God is our refuge and strength, an ever-present help in trouble. Therefore we will not fear, though the earth give way and the mountains fall into the heart of the sea, though its waters roar and foam and the mountains quake with their surging. He says, 'Be still, and know that I am God; I will be exalted among the nations, I will be exalted in the earth.'” —Psalm 46:1-3, 10

REFLECTION:

FEAR II

⚙

Fear is a curse of the world. Fight it like you would a plague. Fear is everywhere, but turn it out of your life. Don't entertain it.

Fear destroys hope—and hope is necessary.

Fear and worry tormented you because of your lack of communion with Me.

- You were worried about exposure of past failures, relationships, and choices.
- You were worried about your future and about what would happen.

Fear and worry are the same bedfellows. They always go together.

Fear and worry make you nervous and paranoid. As you surrender your fears and worries to Me and choose faith over fear, you will find peace that the human mind cannot understand. That peace radiates and draws others to Me.

⚙

"So do not fear, for I am with you; do not be dismayed, for I am your God. I will strengthen you and help you; I will uphold you with my righteous right hand."—Isaiah 41:10

REFLECTION:

FEELING INADEQUATE

෧෨

I am your healer and your strength.

You don't have to ask Me to come to you.

I am always with you.

At your moment of need, I'm here to help you.

Your need is My opportunity.

Rely on My strength whenever you need it. When you feel inadequate to any situation, you should realize that this feeling is disloyalty to Me. Just say to yourself: "I know that God is with me and will help me to think and say and do the right thing."

Don't ever feel inadequate to any situation.

෧෨

"The LORD is my rock, my fortress and my deliverer; my God is my rock, in whom I take refuge, my shield and the horn of my salvation. He is my stronghold, my refuge and my savior— from violent people you save me. I called to the LORD, who is worthy of praise, and have been saved from my enemies." —2 Samuel 22:2-4

REFLECTION:

FILLING OF MY SPIRIT

ೞ

As you rid yourself of fears, resentments, worries, hates, and selfishness, you will make room for My Spirit.

Ask for My Holy Spirit to fill you. A calm will come to your life. Calm comes after a storm. Joy will come to your heart. Birds always sing after a storm. My love and peace and calm will be your new normal. Clean your life of evil so good may come in.

Refilling of My Spirit is something that needs doing every day. You need these times of quiet communion, away, alone, without noise and without activity. You need this dwelling apart, this shutting yourself away alone with your Maker. You will come forth from this communion with new power. This refilling will produce effective work and there will be nothing too hard for you.

ೞ

"But the fruit of the Spirit is love, joy, peace, forbearance, kindness, goodness, faithfulness, gentleness and self-control."
—Galatians 5:22-23

"Do not get drunk on wine, which leads to debauchery. Instead, be filled with the Spirit ..."
—Ephesians 5:18

REFLECTION:

FOCUS

❦

Your focus on or in life is changing. By keeping your thoughts directed toward Me, and including Me in all of your thoughts, you are beginning to realize that I am good. You are looking for good in every situation and you are seeing My presence, even in devastating circumstances. You were blind to My presence previously.

I am love.

I am good.

I am compassion.

I am kind.

I am gentle.

I am all powerful.

I am courage.

You are looking at life with the eyes of faith.

❦

". . .fixing our eyes on Jesus, the pioneer and perfecter of faith. For the joy set before him he endured the cross, scorning its shame, and sat down at the right hand of the throne of God." —Hebrews 12:2

REFLECTION:

FORGIVENESS

୧୫୬

When you repent, I forgive you of *all* of your iniquities. You can believe I have forgiven you of all past sins and new ones, too.

I want you to live today the way I want you to live. Wipe the slate clean of the past and don't go there with regret again. Start today with a clean slate and go forward with confidence.

I have a plan for you and it is good. Go forward, not backwards.

Remember, if My forgiveness were only for the righteous and those who had not sinned, why would it be needed?

Be very grateful for my forgiveness.

୧୫୬

"Who forgives [every one of] all your iniquities, Who heals [each one of] all your diseases. . ." —Psalm 103:3 AMP

REFLECTION:

FORGIVING OTHERS

∞

Forgive those who have hurt you. Don't carry the weight and burden of unforgiveness.

Most of those who hurt you did it unknowingly. If they did it knowingly, forgive them, anyway. Hurting people hurt people.

Forgiveness is My way. Follow Me.

Forgiveness is impossible without Me.

Unforgiveness will keep you away from peace.

Selfishness blocks forgiveness.

In order to have the life I died for, you must forgive. When you really forgive, you won't think about the offense or mention it again. Your thought of the wrongs means you are still in the foreground. Choose to forgive and give Me your life and your will, one day at a time. I want you to walk in peace and contentment daily.

You've got Me.

I want you to hold no resentments. Let Me wash your mind clean of all past hurts and fears.

CℬℰƆ

"For if you forgive other people when they sin against you, your heavenly Father will also forgive you." —Matthew 6:14

REFLECTION:

Forgiving Yourself

⋘⋙

Forgiving yourself is the hardest. Pride blocks you from forgiving yourself.

If you have asked Me for forgiveness and I have wiped your slate clean with this issue, do you think you are above Me?

Forgive yourself.

Talk it through. If the unforgiving thought returns, forgive yourself again and again and again until it torments you no more.

I love you.

⋘⋙

*"Brothers and sisters, I do not consider myself yet to have taken hold of it. But one thing I do: Forgetting what is behind and straining toward what is ahead, I press on toward the goal to win the prize for which God has called me heavenward in Christ Jesus." —*Philippians 3:13-14

REFLECTION:

FREE RENT

❦

When others treat you unfairly or say hurtful things to you, don't obsess about what they did and how you are going to fix it or set the record straight. Their opinion of you isn't important. All that matters is what you think of them.

This situation is the opportunity for you to grow in grace. See how quickly you can forgive the person who wounded you. Bless that person with your thoughts and words. You won't understand why that person is the way he is, but I see and know all things.

Don't give someone who hurts you free rent in your mind.
Keep your focus on Me.

❦

"Bear with each other and forgive one another if any of you has a grievance against someone. Forgive as the Lord forgave you. And over all these virtues put on love, which binds them all together in perfect unity."
—Colossians 3:13-14

REFLECTION:

FREE WILL

ଓଚ୍ଚ

I have given you free will. This is the choice to be on the good side or the bad side, the right side or wrong side.

I am the force in the world for good. You can call this "God's Will." My Will has a wonderful purpose for your life to give you a hope and a future.

If you will give Me your will and ask that My Will be done in your life, you will flow in the stream of goodness in life. You will be on My side and I will be on your side.

Bring all your desires to Me and ask that My Will be done. Do this each day, and then stay out of My business and watch Me work. I will guide you each day.

Before giving Me your will and trusting that My Will will be done every day, you considered yourself brave and independent and a risk taker. Because you weren't relying on Me totally, you were always courting disaster.

I'm so glad you've discovered the sincere prayer, "Not My Will but Thy Will be done." My power is available for you to do the right thing.

ଓଚ୍ଚ

"May the God of hope fill you with all joy and
peace as you trust in him, so that you may

overflow with hope by the power of the Holy Spirit."—Romans 15:13

REFLECTION:

FRIENDS

⚘

Friends are people you can help and who can help you live
a better life.
Don't hold back. Go halfway to be met halfway.
Good friends are a gift not to be taken lightly.

Friends are not people to be used for pleasure or profit.
I will give you friends who understand you and who you
understand. They will be there for you during the worst of
times. Value them.
Remember:

- Real human friendship is based on unselfishness and
  a desire to help each other.
- Friendships in sin are based on selfishness, on people
  using people for their own pleasure.

I extend My hand and invite you to be My friend.
As I am your friend, you will become a friend to others.
I am a friend who is tireless, selfless, all-conquering, and
miracle-working.
Take My hand in yours.

⚘

*"I no longer call you servants, because a
servant does not know his master's business.*

Instead, I have called you friends, for every-thing that I learned from my Father I have made known to you." —John 15:15

"Perfume and incense bring joy to the heart, and the pleasantness of a friend springs from their heartfelt advice." —Proverbs 27:9

REFLECTION:

FRIENDS AND FELLOWSHIP

෴

I don't want you to be a hermit. You need fellowship with others in My family. Spiritual fellowship is important to your well-being. You will have a common belief in God and a desire to live the spiritual life. I will be in the midst of the gathering.

You will also be led to those who don't know Me. You can love them with My love.

Your life will be a light.

෴

"For where two or three gather in my name, there am I with them." —Matthew 18:20

". . . Let your light shine before others, that they may see your good deeds and glorify your Father in heaven." —Matthew 5:16

REFLECTION:

GIVING

Giving of advice can never take the place of giving of yourself.

Live to give.

Give wherever I lead you to give. Giving is a part of your abundant life.

Give your loved ones to Me. I gave them to you to share your life, but remember—they belong to Me, not you. Open your heart and give them back to Me. Place them in My hands, and then place your hand in Mine.

I promise I will walk with you and your loved ones through all that life brings.

CRWO

"Give, and it will be given to you. A good measure, pressed down, shaken together and running over, will be poured into your lap."—Luke 6:38

REFLECTION:

GOAL

⋐ℰ⋑

Your goal is to reach forward and upward to things of the Spirit. Your whole character will change as you do this.

Reach for love,
  For honesty,
    For purity,
      For unselfishness,
        And for true beauty.

Your whole nature will change and you will be able to delight in the abundant life.

Let's talk about your earthly goals—the good life while on earth. What do you want to be like the day you are taken to heaven in these areas? Answering that question will help you set your long-term goals in these aspects of your life and in others:

Financially,
  Mentally,
    Physically,
      Socially,
        Spiritually.

As you work toward each one daily, you are also working on your short-term goals. Knowing you are working on both will be satisfying and give you confidence.

掘

"... *Whatever is true, whatever is noble, whatever is right, whatever is pure, whatever is lovely, whatever is admirable—if anything is excellent or praiseworthy—think about such things."—Philippians 4:8*

REFLECTION:

GOD'S WILL

CRRO

Simple acceptance of My Will is the key to a peaceful life. I know everything and I know what's best for you. Give every situation to Me and say, "Thy Will be done." Accept the outcome as My best for you.

Remember: The timing is up to Me and the outcome
is up to Me.
Trust Me. This is the key to abundant living.

CRRO

"I desire to do your will, my God; your law is within my heart." —Psalm 40:8

"As for God, his way is perfect: The LORD's word is flawless; he shields all who take refuge in him." —Psalm 18:30

REFLECTION:

GOSSIP

౸৪౹

Sow peace and not discord wherever you go.
Try to be a part of the solution of every situation instead of part of the problem.
Always try to build up and never tear down.
Live the right away. The example of what you do says more than what you say.
Be careful with your thinking. Be constructive and choose the good in your thought life.
Say, "But for the grace of God, there go I."
Gossip and criticism of others have no place in your life.
You and I know there is no way you can understand some decisions made by others. Don't even try. Drop it and move on, going forward with Me in your life. Gossip doesn't help anybody.

౸৪౹

"With the tongue we praise our Lord and Father, and with it we curse human beings, who have been made in God's likeness. Out of the same mouth come praise and cursing. My brothers and sisters, this should not be."
—James 3:8-10

REFLECTION:

GRACE

໕໖໔

Your life is a demonstration of what My grace can do. Others will see in you what the working out of My Will does.

My grace in you helps those around you.

Your own pride and selfishness block the way to My grace in you. Keep these out of the way and My grace will flow through you to others. When you do this, all who come in contact with you will be helped in some way.

You've received My grace.
Now you are a giver of My grace.

You can always look at others and say, "But for the grace of God there go I." Don't forget where you would be if it weren't for My grace. Be grateful for My grace.

Do you want the best of life? Then live close to Me because I am the giver of life. My grace and strength will help you conquer life with renewed power. You'll receive power to overcome wrong thinking and you will see others' lives changed through the changes already accomplished in yours. Whatever the changes they see, it is the working of My grace.

My grace is manifest in your life by your power to overcome, your love for other people, your peace of mind, and ethical actions and reactions that display your good character. You have plenty of grace—just ask Me for it each day. Be grateful for My grace.

Set your hopes on My grace. Know that your future holds more and more good. Just keep focused on growing spiritually and rely on My power to do it. Don't focus on material stuff because that just bogs you down.

Come into my arms and let Me love you. You were made righteous through my Son. You can stop beating yourself up. I want you to learn to love yourself, and you start by loving Me.

✂∞

"But he said to me, 'My grace is sufficient for you, for my power is made perfect in weakness.' Therefore I will boast all the more gladly about my weaknesses, so that Christ's power may rest on me." —2 Corinthians 12:9

"Let us then approach God's throne of grace with confidence, so that we may receive mercy and find grace to help us in our time of need." —Hebrews 4:16

REFLECTION:

GRATITUDE

ᘓᙄ

You are learning to be thankful for the important things:

- My grace and mercy,
- Faith,
- Family,
- Friends,
- A roof over your head,
- Food to eat.

These are all gifts. My grace is sufficient.

Your true gratitude to Me for all the blessings I give you puts you on a firm foundation. The other part of the foundation is your true humility because of your unworthiness to receive these blessings. They are gifts you have not earned. Gratitude brings humility.

Be grateful for the things you have received. Saying "thank you" on a daily basis is a must in order to renew your mind. Being thankful is so important.

Thank Me on the grayest days.

ᘓᙄ

". . . give thanks in all circumstances; for this is God's will for you in Christ Jesus."
—1 Thessalonians 5:18

REFLECTION:

Gratitude II

What does "Praise the Lord" mean? It means being grateful for this beautiful universe created by God and grateful for all the blessings in your life and all the gray days:

- If you didn't have sadness, how would you know joy?
- If you didn't have sin, how would you know righteousness?
- If you didn't know bondage, how would you appreciate freedom?
- If you didn't know lack, how would you recognize My sufficiency?
- If you didn't know strife, how could you appreciate peace?

Gratitude coupled with humility is powerful. You won't be as tempted to do wrong and you will have a feeling of security because you will be looking to Me and praising God. Humility comes from knowing and remembering that you didn't do anything to deserve My blessings.

Be grateful for My Spirit in you, which gives you strength to overcome. My Spirit is powerful and He can help you live a conquering, abundant life.

"Through Jesus, therefore, let us continually offer to God a sacrifice of praise —the fruit of lips that openly profess his name."
—Hebrews 13:15

REFLECTION:

Guidance

༃

The plan of your life is in My mind. When we are in quiet communion and you are meditating—listening to Me—you can seek My plan for your day. Then you can live your day according to My direction and guidance.

Follow My divine intent for your life today.

Choose the right thing when you have choices to make. When you do, you will feel My power supporting you.

I will guide you to the right decisions when you pray about them. Pray to be shown the right way to live today.

As you go about your day, pay attention to your conscience. Follow its leading.

See today's events and interruptions as My leading, planning, and ordering. Remember: My ways are not your ways. I will lead you to the right decision. Wait until you know which way to go. Carry out My guidance as best as you can. I will always guide you to do the right thing. Your conscience will be clear and that is the indication that you have done My Will in any given situation. Leave the results and timing to Me, and it will be all right. This is where you exercise your faith in Me. I know your circumstances, your individual life, your character, your capabilities and your weaknesses.

Trust Me.

And never leave until tomorrow the thing that you are guided to do today.

൚

"You came near when I called you, and you said, 'Do not fear.'" —Lamentations3:57

"Who is going to harm you if you are eager to do good? But even if you should suffer for what is right, you are blessed. "Do not fear their threats[1]; do not be frightened." But in your hearts revere Christ as Lord. Always be prepared to give an answer to everyone who asks you to give the reason for the hope that you have." —1 Peter 3:13-15

REFLECTION:

GUIDANCE II

၁၈၀

Your attitude of "Thy Will be done, and not mine" leads to clear guidance. In quiet times of communion with Me, if you have this attitude you will get that clear guidance. Act on it and you will be led to better things.

Your impulses are lessening and My Spirit is leading your thoughts more and more. Obeying My Will is going to bring answers to your prayers.

You can depend on Me to show you what to do and to give you the strength to do it.

၁၈၀

"The one who calls you is faithful, and he will do it." —1 Thessalonians 5:24

"Your word is a lamp for my feet, a light on my path." —Psalm 119:105

REFLECTION:

GUILT

⚜

Guilt isn't from Me when you are My child.
Guilt weighs you down like quicksand.

You will be convicted of sin because I love you. When you stumble and sometimes fall, come to Me and let Me forgive you, pick you up, and brush you off. I will bind up your wounds and heal you. When you fall, run to Me as fast as you can.

Everybody has sinned. You are not the only one. Shift your focus ahead and keep going forward. Forgive yourself. Don't look back and get caught up in guilt and shame.

Handle your shortcomings with integrity and character.
Ask for forgiveness.
Learn from your mistakes and go forward.

⚜

". . . for all have sinned and fall short of the glory of God, and all are justified freely by his grace through the redemption that came by Christ Jesus." —Romans 3:23-24

REFLECTION:

HAPPINESS

C38O

You can't find true happiness by searching for it. It doesn't come through accumulation of things or fleeting happenings.

Seeking happiness does not *find* happiness, only disillusionment. Seeking pleasure doesn't find happiness.

Happiness is the by-product of living the right kind of life and doing the right thing. True happiness comes as a result of living the right kind of life the way you believe I want you to live regarding Me, yourself, and others.

Don't have pleasure as your goal.

Have knowing Me as your goal and you will find happiness.

When you do the right thing, happiness will come.

Selfishly seeking pleasure doesn't bring true happiness.

CR8O

"He has shown you, O mortal, what is good. And what does the LORD require of you? To act justly and to love mercy and to walk humbly with your God." —Micah 6:8

REFLECTION:

HELP

CRITICAL

Remember, I chose you.

I will help you.

I called you.

I am faithful.

I will do it.

When I hear you cry, "Jesus, help me!" I hear you. At that instant the battle becomes mine. Just simply trust Me as I fight for you. My peace will wash all the irritants away.

CRITICAL

"You did not choose me, but I chose you and appointed you so that you might go and bear fruit—fruit that will last—and so that whatever you ask in my name the Father will give you."—John 15:16

"Keep your lives free from the love of money and be content with what you have, because God has said, 'Never will I leave you; never will I forsake you.' So we say with confidence, 'The Lord is my helper; I will not be afraid. What can mere mortals do to me?'"
—Hebrews 13:5-6

"And I will ask the Father, and he will give you another advocate to help you and be with you forever. . ."—John 14:16

"The one who calls you is faithful, and he will do it."—1 Thessalonians 5:24

REFLECTION:

HELP II

ॐ

Ask for help for each twenty-four hours.

You have to admit your helplessness before I answer your cry for help. Recognize your need before you ask Me to meet that need. Once you recognize your need and pray to Me, I hear you above every sound in heaven.

Your sincere soul cry for help is heard and will be answered.

It's certain.

I will help you through weakness to power,

through danger to security,

through fear and worry to peace and serenity.

You are making progress and going forward as you take My help.

ॐ

"Have mercy on me, my God, have mercy on me, for in you I take refuge. I will take refuge in the shadow of your wings until the disaster has passed.

"I cry out to God Most High, to God, who vindicates me. He sends from heaven and saves me, rebuking those who hotly pursue

me—God sends forth his love and his faith-fulness."—Psalm 57:1-3

"I lift up my eyes to the mountains—where does my help come from?"—Psalm 121:1

"When I called, you answered me, you greatly emboldened me."—Psalm 138:3

REFLECTION:

HELPING OTHERS

Help others all you can. Every troubled soul I put in your path is one for you to help. As you try to help, a supply of strength will flow in to you from Me.

I will hand out the spiritual food to you and you pass it on. Your circle of helpfulness will widen more and more. Don't ever say you only have enough strength for your own need.

When you are helping others, avoid criticism, blame, and judgment. To be effective you need to control your emotions. Humility, drawn from your spiritual foundation, is the key. If you go easy on them and hard on yourself when you share, it will benefit them the most.

- Build them up instead of tearing them down.
- Seek no personal recognition for being used by Me to help others.

You have a purpose in life and you are worth something. You can do something—and that is to help others. I brought you through hazards of life to real usefulness in the world.

I have let you live for this. Your opportunity and destiny is to help others.

Keep pouring yourself out to help others and I will keep filling you up with My Spirit.

"For the whole Law [concerning human relationships] is complied with in the one precept, You shall love your neighbor as [you do] yourself." —Galatians 5:14

". . . .My cup overflows." —Psalm 23:5b

REFLECTION:

HONESTY

༺༻

Quit lying. Stop trying to impress others. You are not perfect and no one else is, either.

You've had some downs in life but so has everyone else. I want you to learn to be honest. No more ducking and dodging. Quit stretching the truth.

Remember, I love you and I know you. What can man do to you?

Quit trying to be somebody you're not. Be who I made you to be and don't be apologetic about it. Honesty is a big part of mental health.

༺༻

"But let your 'Yes' be 'Yes,' and your 'No,' 'No.'" –Matthew 5:37

"So we say with confidence, 'The Lord is my helper; I will not be afraid. What can mere mortals do to me?'" —Hebrews 13:6

REFLECTION:

HOPE

CR80

Since your intimate communion with Me began, what has happened to you?

- Selflessness and cooperation have blossomed.
- Understanding has replaced misunderstanding, blaming, and resentment.
- You are living in peace and hope.
- You are trusting My Will.
- You have grown in faith.
- You don't know how My plans are laid but you know I am working all things together for your good and My glory.
- You've learned one day at a time is enough for you.
- You are learning to set your hope on My goodness and grace.

Set your hopes on spiritual things because an abundance of material things can wear you down. Spiritual things have the higher value.

Never forget: All things are possible with Me.

CR80

"For the LORD *will be your confidence, and will keep your foot from being caught."* — Proverbs 3:26

"For the grace of God has appeared that offers salvation to all people. It teaches us to say 'No' to ungodliness and worldly passions, and to live self-controlled, upright and godly lives in this present age, while we wait for the blessed hope—the appearing of the glory of our great God and Savior, Jesus Christ...—Titus 2:11-13

"May the God of hope fill you with all joy and peace as you trust in him, so that you may overflow with hope by the power of the Holy Spirit."—Romans 15:13

"God is our refuge and strength, an ever-present help in trouble."—Psalm 46:1

REFLECTION:

Humility

I want you to balance true humility and self-respect.

You have learned humility through failures. Not until you have failed can you learn true humility. Failures have taught you that you are no better than anyone else. You are grateful to Me for giving you the strength to rise above past failures.

Now I want you to have self-respect, respect for others, and yet be humble. You can be tolerant of others' failings and not have a critical attitude toward them. I can give you the strength and wisdom to do this.

There is power in humility. True humility is not weakness. Stay humble, knowing you didn't do anything to deserve My blessings.

"Humility is the fear of the Lord; its wages are riches and honor and life."—Proverbs 22:4

"Humble yourselves, therefore, under God's mighty hand, that he may lift you up in due time".—1 Peter 5:5-6

"But he gives us more grace. That is why Scripture says: 'God opposes the proud but gives grace to the humble.'" —James 4:6, quoting Proverbs 3:34

"Though the LORD is on high, he looks upon the lowly, but the proud he knows from afar." —Psalm 138:6

REFLECTION:

HURTS

CREO

When you are hurt, don't respond to emotional upset with emotional upset.

Keep calm in all circumstances. Don't fight back. Call on My grace to help you when you are hurt and feel like retaliating. Resentments drag you down.

Look to Me. If you are burdened by annoyances, you will lose your inward peace. You do not want to lose your peace. Do things that will make peace.

CREO

"Blessed are the peacemakers, for they will be called sons of God." — Matthew 5:9

REFLECTION:

HURTFUL LIVING

☙

Stop doing the things that hurt you over and over again. To do this you will have to change your thinking.

☙

"Now if I do what I do not want to do, it is no longer I who do it, but it is sin living in me that does it. So I find this law at work: When I want to do good, evil is right there with me. For in my inner being I delight in God's law; but I see another law at work in the members of my body, waging war against the law of my mind and making me a prisoner of the law of sin at work within my members. What a wretched man I am! Who will rescue me from this body of death? Thanks be to God—through Jesus Christ our Lord!" —Romans 7:20-25

REFLECTION:

INADEQUACY

౧౩౮౦

Your need is My opportunity.

I am your healer and your strength. I am your shepherd and I will guide you. I am your wisdom.

You don't have to ask Me to come to you because I am always with you in spirit. At your moment of need I am there to help you.

Rely on My strength, or what you need, when you need it.

Have you thought that a feeling of inadequacy could be considered disloyalty to Me?

Just say to yourself: "I know God is with me and will help me think and say and do the right thing."

God is for me.

Jesus is with me.

His Holy Spirit is in me.

I am adequate to any situation."

౧౩౮౦

"No one will be able to stand against you all the days of your life. As I was with Moses, so I will be with you; I will never leave you nor forsake you." —Joshua 1:5

REFLECTION

INFERIORITY COMPLEX

❦

Your inferiority complex is self-centered.

You have been full of self-pity. These feelings cause you to shy away from responsibilities in life.

You are not a victim anymore! You are a victor with Me.

Commune with Me one day at a time and I will free you from inferiority and self-centeredness.

I want you to throw your shoulders back and look everyone in the face knowing that you are loved.

Building yourself up to others was a defense against your feelings of inferiority. You don't need to do that anymore because you are so secure in our relationship.

❦

"You give me your shield of victory, and your right hand sustains me; you stoop down to make me great." —Psalm 18:35

REFLECTION:

INNER CONFLICTS

☙❧

You are getting rid of most of your inner conflicts. You were so hard on yourself. Always putting yourself down. Comparing your very worst with someone else's very best. Your personality was wrapped up in how you thought you appeared to others—what you thought others were thinking of you and your reaction to what you thought others were thinking.

Now you know this thinking is absurd. Now your thinking is getting sorted out because you are giving Me your life and your will on a daily basis and asking for My Will to be done that day. Your thinking has come around to loving Me, being aware of My presence, and loving others. You are no longer going against your conscience.

You were conflicted because you were pleasing others and wanting their acceptance and approval. You are no longer going against your inner voice. You're no longer thinking you have to be perfect.

☙❧

"If any of you lacks wisdom, you should ask God, who gives generously to all without finding fault, and it will be given to you. But when you ask, you must believe and

not doubt, because the one who doubts is like a wave of the sea, blown and tossed by the wind. That person should not expect to receive anything from the Lord. Such a person is double-minded and unstable in all they do." —James 1:5-8

REFLECTION:

INSTABILITY

CBEO

Sometimes you quit living one day at a time and you begin to get unstable because your life is made up of many complex components: family life, job, physical health, spiritual health, emotional state, present circumstances, past experiences, friends, hobbies, hope for the future, and your relationship with Me.

It's easy to feel fragmented and unstable unless you realize that I've only created you to bear twenty-four hours.

Live one day at a time.

Realize I see the big picture as a complicated jigsaw puzzle of your life. Each component is a piece of the puzzle. Keep your eyes, thoughts, and heart set on Me because I will complete the puzzle on my timetable and according to My Will for your life.

Trust Me.

CBEO

"Trust in the LORD with all your heart and lean not on your own understanding. In all

*your ways submit to him, and he will make
your paths straight."* —Proverbs 3:5-6

"Blessed is the man who makes the LORD *his
trust, who does not look to the proud, to those
who turn aside to false gods."* —Psalm 40:4

*"'For I know the plans I have for you,'
declares the* LORD, *'plans to prosper you and
not to harm you, plans to give you hope and a
future.'"* —Jeremiah 29:11

REFLECTION:

I WILL KEEP YOU

CRUD

You will be kept by My grace and mercy. Don't doubt that My Spirit is always with you, wherever you are, to keep you on the right path. My keeping power is never at fault—only your realization of it. You must believe in My nearness.

A daily quiet communion time with Me is a must. Our communion keeps you balanced and going forward.

I am your security.
I am your everything.

Your security is in Me—not in anything that can be taken away.

Lift up your eyes and thoughts from the impure, repulsive, and morally degrading things on earth and look to Me. I made the heavens and earth and I will keep you from all evil.

I will keep your going in and coming out from this day forward and for evermore. Trust Me wholly.

Practice saying, "It will all be okay."

CRUD

"I lift up my eyes to the hills—where does my help come from? My help comes from the

LORD, the Maker of heaven and earth. He will not let your foot slip—he who watches over you will not slumber; indeed, he who watches over Israel will neither slumber nor sleep. The LORD watches over you—the LORD is your shade at your right hand; the sun will not harm you by day, nor the moon by night. The LORD will keep you from all harm—he will watch over your life; the LORD will watch over your coming and going both now and forevermore." —Psalm 121

REFLECTION:

JEALOUSY

Lose jealousy. It's a barrier to My grace. It separates you and Me and it separates you from others. It impedes your progress in going forward.

Don't entertain jealousy. Recognize immediately that it is your enemy.

"Let us behave decently, as in the day-time . . . not in dissension and jealousy."
—Romans 13:13

"The acts of the flesh are obvious: sexual immorality, impurity and debauchery; idolatry and witchcraft; hatred, discord, jealousy, fits of rage, selfish ambition, dissensions, factions and envy; drunkenness, orgies, and the like. I warn you, as I did before, that those who live like this will not inherit the kingdom of God." —Galatians 5:19-21

REFLECTION:

JUDGING OTHERS

∽§∾

You are learning not to judge others.

If your life were held under a microscope for all to see, it would not be perfect. Exactly the opposite. You've made a lot of wrong choices and taken a lot of wrong paths. You've learned that when you have judged people, so often you are wrong.

Don't look at the toothpick in their eye when you have a log in your own.

Only I know another person's mind and heart. I am each one's Maker. Each mind is different, moved by different motives, controlled by different circumstances and influenced by different sufferings. You don't know what another person has been through.

You won't ever understand everything and you are not better than other good people. Your life has just had a different path than theirs. You can't afford to be critical and intolerant of people, because you will lose your peace. Put them in My hands and let go. Pray "Thy Will be done."

Don't be "holier than thou." You don't have all the answers. When you are free of this judgmental attitude, you can focus on our relationship and our eternal life together.

∽§∾

"Do not judge, and you will not be judged. Do not condemn, and you will not be condemned. Forgive, and you will be forgiven."—Luke 6:37

REFLECTION:

LAWS OF LIFE

ങ്ങ

I created laws of nature and moral and spiritual laws. Submit to these laws and stay healthy.

You are not an exception. These apply to everyone. When you choose to break these laws, you will suffer the consequences.

Pray that you will stay true to the laws of honesty, purity, unselfishness, and love.

Live in harmony with My laws. I will give you the strength and power to do this.

ങ്ങ

"Righteous are you, O LORD, and your laws are right. The statutes you have laid down are righteous; they are fully trustworthy."
—Psalm 119 (*Tsadhe*):137-138

REFLECTION:

LIFE

⊂℥⊃

Life is a school.
Spend time with Me and I will teach you.
Read the Bible, My Word. It is full of wisdom.
Listen and I will speak to your mind and heart.
Be persistent.

Make a habit of our heart-to-heart communication. I will reveal Myself to you.

Make it a practice to do what you learn. Learning without doing is not learning at all.

⊂℥⊃

"Do not merely listen to the word, and so deceive yourselves. Do what it says."
—James 1:22

REFLECTION:

LISTEN

⊂⊃

Listen for the still small voice in your quiet times. It's Me.

I am your shepherd and you are My sheep. You will know My voice.

- Be a good listener with others.
- Don't dominate the conversation.
- Don't interrupt.
- Hear people.

I will empower your listening if you ask Me to.

⊂⊃

" . . . and after the earthquake a fire, but the LORD was not in the fire; and after the fire a still small voice." — 1 Kings 19:12 NKJV

"When he has brought out all his own, he goes on ahead of them, and his sheep follow him because they know his voice. . . .'I am the good shepherd; I know my sheep and my sheep know me.'" — John 10: 4, 14

REFLECTION:

LOVE

⚛

I have given you love
　Love for Me,
　　Love for others,
　　　And love for yourself.
　This love is unselfish and has an outgoing desire to help others. Doing what's best for the other person above your own desires is this kind of love. This kind of love is gentle, kind, and understanding.

　　What you do for yourself is lost,
　　But what you do for others is written in eternity.

　Love and fear cannot dwell together. A strong love for Me will dispel fear. Fear will flee.
　My love for you is never ending.
　Love is the power that transformed your life. Love your family and friends—everybody. You are sowing My life into their lives when you do this.

　　Sprinkle My love on everyone.

Love for Me is the greater call for you. This love is the result of your gratitude and acknowledgement of the blessings I've sent you.

ॐ

"And now these three remain: faith, hope and love. But the greatest of these is love."
— 1 Corinthians 13:13

"Jesus replied: "'Love the Lord your God with all your heart and with all your soul and with all your mind.' This is the first and greatest commandment. And the second is like it: "'Love your neighbor as yourself.'"
—Matthew 22:37-39

REFLECTION:

LOVING OTHERS

⊙₰⊙

You have become less negative and more positive. Instead of being so negative and distrustful of others, you are seeing others as I see them. Everyone has a different path and I am drawing them to Me.

- Take a real interest in others.
- Have a real desire to help.
- Become less sensitive and focused on yourself.
- Seek friendships by at least going halfway.
- Become less self-centered, knowing the world doesn't revolve around you in its center.
- Build up instead of tearing down.

Love others and look over their faults. Practice this and use My strength to do it. See good in all people, those you like and those who go against your grain.

Love means no severe judging, no resentments, no malicious gossip, and no destructive criticism. It means patience, understanding, compassion, and helpfulness.

I can bring you to loving others and loving yourself.

Trust Me.

⊙₰⊙

"A new command I give you: Love one another. As I have loved you, so you must love one another. By this everyone will know that you are my disciples, if you love one another." —John 13:34-35

REFLECTION:

LYING

⚮

Don't get in the habit of lying. Lying causes fear because you will always have the fear of being found out.

Tell the truth. Living in truth gives you peace.

⚮

"Simply let your 'Yes' be 'Yes,' and your 'No,' 'No'; anything beyond this comes from the evil one." —Matthew 5:37

REFLECTION:

MATERIAL THINGS

CRESO

Don't let material things choke out spiritual things. Functioning solely on a material plane will take you away from Me. Functioning on a spiritual plane as well as a material plane will make life what it should be.

CRESO

"With me are riches and honor, enduring wealth and prosperity." —Proverbs 8:18 NIV

"A good name is more desirable than great riches; to be esteemed is better than silver or gold." —Proverbs 22:1

"'Let not the wise boast of their wisdom or the strong boast of their strength or the rich boast of their riches, but let the one who boasts boast about this: that they have the understanding to know me, that I am the LORD, who exercises kindness, justice and righteousness on earth, for in these I delight,' declares the LORD." —Jeremiah 9:23-24

REFLECTION:

MEANING OF LIFE

☙

I am life.

I am the meaning of life.

It is a waste of time to seek for the meaning outside Me.

Don't be drawn in and influenced by any other philosophy. It will be based on human tradition or world principles.

Everything is held together by Me.
Is your life falling apart? Come to Me.

Are you seeking eternal life? Eternity is not only for those who will spend it in heaven. There are many who are eternally in hell and they will be there forever.

Eternal life is knowing Me.
To know the Father is to know the Son.
Eternal life is knowing Me, Jesus.
It's that simple.

☙

"He is before all things, and in him all things hold together." —Colossians 1:17

"I am the resurrection and the life. He who believes in me will live, even though he dies." —John 11:25

"I am the way and the truth and the life. No one comes to the Father except through me." —John 14:6

"See to it that no one takes you captive through hollow and deceptive philosophy, which depends on human tradition and the basic principles of this world rather than on Christ. For in Christ all the fullness of the Deity lives in bodily form . . ." —Colossians 2:8-9

"Now this is eternal life: that they may know you, the only true God, and Jesus Christ, whom you have sent." —John 17:3

"Here I am! I stand at the door and knock. If anyone hears my voice and opens the door, I will come in and eat with that person, and they with me." —Mark 16:16

"Peter replied, 'Repent and be baptized, every one of you, in the name of Jesus Christ for the forgiveness of your sins. And you will receive the gift of the Holy Spirit.'" —Acts 2:38

CRSD

PRAYER TO BECOME A CHRISTIAN:

Dear God, I repent of my sins. I ask You to forgive me.
Lord Jesus, I ask You to come into my heart and be my
Lord and Savior.

—Amen

REFLECTION:

MEDITATION

ⳡ

In quiet times of meditation you are learning to hear My voice. I speak to your heart and give you peace. I speak to you intimately and personally as we spend quiet time together.

I am like a lamp to your feet and a light to your path.

You are learning during these quiet times to set your hope on My grace. Know that your future holds more and more good.

You really listen to Me when you are desperate. I am moved by your desperate, humble cry. Listening quietly and knowing My presence is with you is what it's all about.

You can't lose by listening for My voice. When we are alone say, "Speak Lord. I'm ready to listen." Even if you aren't aware that I've spoken to your heart, you will see the fruit.

I talk to you because I love you. Draw into that secret place where you and I communicate and let Me love you.

ⳡ

"Be still, and know that I am God; I will be exalted among the nations, I will be exalted in the earth." —Psalm 46:10

"May my meditation be pleasing to him, as I rejoice in the LORD." —Psalm 104:34

"Your word is a lamp to my feet and a light for my path." —Psalm 119:105 *(Nun)*

"For these commands are a lamp, this teaching is a light, and the corrections of discipline are the way to life." —Proverbs 6:23

REFLECTION:

MEDITATION II

03&O

Life in the Spirit is a calm, peaceful place away from the hubbub of the world. It is full of peace, serenity, and contentment.

When you are meditating in communion with Me in this quiet place in the Spirit, you will draw strength from Me for your day.

Meditating is the practice of improving and reinforcing your conscious contact with Me.

In these quiet times I will teach you how to rest your nerves. Don't be afraid. I will teach you how to relax. As you relax, My peace will flow through.

Hush your mind's connection to the material world and connect with Me.

Ask Me to direct your thinking for the next twenty-four hours. Pray in this way:

"Please show me through the day what my next step will be. Thy Will be done in me and through me today."

03&O

"Blessed is the one who does not walk in step with the wicked or stand in the way that sinners take or sit in the company of mockers, but whose delight is in the law of the LORD,

*and who meditates on his law day and night.
That person is like a tree planted by streams
of water, which yields its fruit in season and
whose leaf does not wither—whatever they
do prospers."*—Psalm 1:1-3

REFLECTION:

MENTAL PUNISHMENT

C38O

What mental punishment you have put yourself through! Your personality has been wrapped up in how you thought you appeared to others, what you thought others were thinking of you, and then you reacted to what you thought others were thinking. When you were in control this is the way you thought.

You now see what punishment this was to yourself and how this is self-centered thinking. You have broken free by surrendering your life and will to Me on a daily basis and asking for My Will to be done during the next twenty-four hours. You don't go there anymore and I'm so proud of you.

You have sought to follow My Spirit and this has reversed unhealthy thinking. This reversal has led to happiness and peace.

Keep it up.

Call on Me.

I'm here for you.

CstO

"For God has not given us a spirit of fear, but of power and of love and of a sound mind." —2 Timothy 1:7 NKJV

"And the peace of God, which transcends all understanding, will guard your hearts and your minds in Christ Jesus." —Philippians 4:7

REFLECTION:

MIRACLES

෮෫ඁ

The greatest miracle is the change in your life and the healing of your mind.

As you trust completely in Me and live one day at a time with My guidance you are becoming whole.

Have faith in My miracle-working power. There is nothing I cannot accomplish in changing your life.

However, don't put your faith in miracles. Put your faith in Me.

෮෫ඁ

"Therefore, if anyone is in Christ, he is a new creation; the old has gone, the new has come!" —2 Corinthians 5:17

REFLECTION:

MISTAKES

C380

You can make use of your mistakes, failures, shortcomings, losses, and sufferings.

It's not what happens to you so much as what you are becoming.

Take these things and use them. Your experience and growth will help others. Others can gain from your experiences and good can come from them.

Say to yourself, "I had to be where I was to be where I am."

C380

"But by the grace of God I am what I am . . ." The apostle Paul in 1 Corinthians 15:10, explaining how, in spite of his background and unworthiness, God has used him.

REFLECTION:

MONEY

⚜

Wasting money puts a burden on your shoulders.

When you come to Me I will guide you on where your money should go. This heavy burden can be lifted from your shoulders. I want you to be released from this burden and walk in freedom. Let Me guide you.

Excess money or riches seem to give people a feeling of pride and importance.
I'm more impressed with humility.

⚜

"Those who love money will never have enough. How meaningless to think that wealth brings true happiness! The more you have, the more people come to help you spend it. So what good is wealth—except perhaps to watch it slip through your fingers!"
—Ecclesiastes 5:10-11 NLT

"For the love of money is a root of all kinds of evil. Some people, eager for money, have

210

wandered from the faith and pierced them-selves with many griefs." — 1 Timothy 6:10a

REFLECTION:

Most Important

൚

The most important decision you have made is giving Me your life and your will and asking that My Will be done each twenty-four hours I give you.

The most important thing now is to stay close to Me. Nothing should be more important than this.

൚

"For God so loved the world that He gave His only begotten Son, that whoever believes in Him should not perish but have everlasting life." —John 3:16 NKJV

"If you declare with your mouth, 'Jesus is Lord,' and believe in your heart that God raised him from the dead, you will be saved." —Romans 10:9

"Therefore, if anyone is in Christ, the new creation has come. The old has gone, the new is here!" —2 Corinthians 5:17

"For it is by grace you have been saved, through faith—and this is not from yourselves,

it is the gift of God—not by works, so that no one can boast. For we are God's handiwork, created in Christ Jesus to do good works, which God prepared in advance for us to do." —Ephesians 2:8-10

"Come near to God and he will come near to you. Wash your hands, you sinners, and purify your hearts, you double-minded." —James 4:8a

"Here I am! I stand at the door and knock. If anyone hears my voice and opens the door, I will come in and eat with that person, and they with me." —Revelation 3:20

REFLECTION:

My Love

☙

Being conscious of My love and presence in your life makes a big difference.

With this consciousness or awareness, you are open to Me and My Will for you.

This *openness* relieves you from the cares and worries of this world.

This *relief* brings peace and contentment.

This *peace* passes all understanding.

This *contentment* can no one take away from you.

You can be sure of My love for you.

☙

"For I am convinced that neither death nor life, neither angels nor demons, neither the present nor the future, nor any powers, neither height nor depth, nor anything else in all creation, will be able to separate us from the love of God that is in Christ Jesus our Lord." —Romans 8:38-39

"See, I have engraved you on the palms of my hands. . ." —Isaiah 49:16a

"Indeed, the very hairs of your head are all numbered. Don't be afraid; you are worth more than many sparrows." —Luke 12:7

"Give thanks to the God of gods. His love endures forever." —Psalm 136:2

*"The L*ORD* appeared to us in the past, saying: 'I have loved you with an everlasting love; I have drawn you with unfailing kindness.'"* —Jeremiah 31:3

REFLECTION:

My Power

ᘖ

As far as spiritual things are concerned, My power is limitless.

You need to realize there are limitations with temporal and material things. For example, you cannot see the road ahead, so you need to go one step at a time.

ᘖ

I don't give you a longer view.
Learn to walk with Me by faith one step at a time, one day at a time.
My Will gives you perfect freedom.
Trust Me.

"He gives power to the weak, And to those who have no might He increases strength."
—Isaiah 40:29 NKJV

"But he said to me, 'My grace is sufficient for you, for my power is made perfect in weakness.' Therefore I will boast all the more gladly about my weaknesses, so that Christ's power may rest on me." —2 Corinthians 12:9

REFLECTION:

MY PRESENCE

CℜℬO

You will find joy in My presence. Real, true joy.

I'm waiting to be with you when you wake up and I'm with you throughout the day and through the night. Be conscious of My presence, because I will never leave you nor forsake you.

Be aware of My presence in every moment of your day. My presence with you is a gift.

Strive to abide in My presence. Learn to live in My presence and then you will have My strength, power, and joy.

I look for the few people who want to be near Me, just to dwell in My presence, not so much for teaching or a message but just for Me. I've found *you*. Live each day and each moment as though you are in My presence because I am with you and I will never leave you.

Don't take a step away from Me toward temptation. Doing that is like making a small hole in a dam to allow sin to come flooding in. If you do make that mistake, run back to Me in repentance to repair the hole.

CℜℬO

"I am the vine; you are the branches. If a man
remains in me and I in him, he will bear much
fruit; apart from me you can do nothing. . .

218

.If you remain in me and my words remain in you, ask whatever you wish, and it will be given you. This is to my Father's glory, that you bear much fruit, showing yourselves to be my disciples. As the Father has loved me, so have I loved you. Now remain in my love." —John 15:5, 7-9

"You have made known to me the path of life; you will fill me with joy in your presence, with eternal pleasures at your right hand." —Psalm 16:11

"One thing I ask from the Lord, this only do I seek: that I may dwell in the house of the Lord all the days of my life, to gaze on the beauty of the Lord and to seek him in his temple. My heart says of you, 'Seek his face!' Your face, Lord, I will seek." —Psalm 27:4, 8

REFLECTION:

MY SPIRIT

୧୫୨୦

Breathe in My Spirit during our communion today and throughout the day.

My Spirit is honesty, purity, unselfishness, and love.

Choose to follow My Spirit these twenty-four hours.

My Spirit is inexhaustible. Share it with others by
helping,
understanding,
giving, and
listening.

Pray while listening and you will stay in communion with My Spirit.

I've given you two great gifts: My Spirit and the power of choice. When you choose selfishness, greed, and pride, you are refusing My Spirit. When you accept love and unselfishness, you are accepting My Spirit.

୧୫୨୦

"Peter replied, 'Repent and be baptized, every one of you, in the name of Jesus Christ for the forgiveness of your sins. And you will receive the gift of the Holy Spirit. The promise is for you and your children and for all who

are far off—for all whom the LORD *our God will call.'"* — Acts 2:38-39

"Do you not know that you are the temple of God and that the Spirit of God dwells in you?" — 1 Corinthians 3:16 NKJV

"This day I call the heavens and the earth as witnesses against you that I have set before you life and death, blessings and curses. Now choose life, so that you and your children may live." — Deuteronomy 30:19

". . . Whatever is true, whatever is noble, whatever is right, whatever is pure, whatever is lovely, whatever is admirable—if anything is excellent or praiseworthy—think about such things." — Philippians 4:9

REFLECTION:

My Will

You have found that seeking My Will brings happiness. To do My Will brings contentment to your soul.

Wanting your way and your will brings discontentment. Taking and not giving doesn't bring good to your life. It's selfish—and selfishness is not good.

Seeking My Will and guidance for the day is going forward in the only life you are given, and that's what life is all about.

When your soul is in union with Me, you get new life, strength, and spiritual power.

Doing My Will is the true meaning of living. Can you say "Thy Will be done" in good times and in bad times? I am walking beyond your understanding and you can trust Me.

My Will won't ever put you where my presence will not sustain you.

Want My Will above all things and help others to find My Will for them.

Pray "Thy Will be done" often. Knowing that My Will is being done should give you gladness. When you live knowing that My Will is being done, everything tends to work out well in the long run. When you are honestly trying to do My Will and humbly accepting the results, nothing can seriously hurt you. When accepting My Will in your life, you will inherit real peace of mind.

I look on your heart and not at your outward appearance. All I am looking for is a simple desire always to do My Will.

ᏣᏃᏦᎠ

"As for God, his way is perfect: the LORD's word is flawless; he shields all who take refuge in him." —Psalm 18:30

"As for you, the anointing you received from him remains in you, and you do not need anyone to teach you. But as his anointing teaches you about all things and as that anointing is real, not counterfeit—just as it has taught you, remain in him." —1 John 2:27

"I desire to do your will, my God; your law is within my heart." —Psalm 40:8

REFLECTION:

NEEDS

I have created you with needs. You need air to breathe, you need food to live. You need water to survive.

You also have a need to be loved. I am love. I supply this need one on one and through others. Your needs are not sin, so don't get them confused with sin. Having needs does not make you weak. I delight in meeting your needs.

You will never outgrow your needs because they are a part of who you are. I desire to liberally supply your every need through My riches.

I created you, and I love you.

Think of Me any way you want to—just know you need Me. Turn to Me in every situation, because I will supply your needs.

When you are weak, you need My strength.

When you are strong, you need My tenderness.

When you are tempted or have fallen, you need My saving grace.

When you are right with Me, you need My pity for sinners.

When you are lonely, you need Me as a friend.

You need My love.

"And my God will meet all your needs according to his glorious riches in Christ Jesus." —Philippians 4:19

" 'No eye has seen, no ear has heard, no mind has conceived what God has prepared for those who love him.' " —1 Corinthians 2:9, quoting Isaiah 64:4

REFLECTION:

NEW LIFE

෴

With this new life of faith in Me, one day at a time you have gotten rid of things such as fears, resentments, inferiority complexes, negative points of view, self-centeredness, critical thoughts of others, over-sensitiveness, inner conflicts, false perfectionism, jealousy and envy, comparing yourself and your life to those of others, and more poisons of the soul.

You are going forward in life by giving Me your life and your will, one day at a time, and asking for My Will to be done that day.

I am proud of you, and I look at you and smile.

෴

"Therefore, if anyone is in Christ, the new creation has come The old has gone, the new is here!" —2 Corinthians 5:17

"For you died, and your life is now hidden with Christ in God. When Christ, who is your life, appears, then you also will appear with him in glory." —Colossians 3:3-4

REFLECTION:

ONE DAY AT A TIME

☙

Learn to live one day at a time. Today is all you have.

Do your best with everything that comes your way. Before the day starts, give it to Me and ask, "Thy Will be done." Through the day give things to Me and ask, "Thy Will be done." Know that every interruption comes because I allowed it.

Your life is a succession of "todays."
What you do on your todays will mold your tomorrows.
Choose well today.

Your future is made up of todays. Your future is no longer hopeless. It will take care of itself because you are living right now, and in the rightness of now.

I am with you and will see you through.

Do not get discouraged. You are too hard on yourself. I am pleased with your progress. I am the judge—not you.

Don't dwell on the past or on the future. Dwell only on the present.

☙

"Therefore do not worry about tomorrow, for tomorrow will worry about itself. Each day has enough trouble of its own."
—Matthew 6:34

"Do not be anxious about anything, but in every situation, by prayer and petition, with thanksgiving, present your requests to God. And the peace of God, which transcends all understanding, will guard your hearts and your minds in Christ Jesus."
—Philippians 4:6-7

"Therefore, there is now no condemnation for those who are in Christ Jesus." —Romans 8:1

"Who will bring any charge against those whom God has chosen? It is God who justifies. Who is he that condemns? Christ Jesus, who died—more than that, who was raised to life—is at the right hand of God and is also interceding for us." —Romans 8:33-34

REFLECTION:

ONE DAY AT A TIME II

୧୫୫୦

I have made you to be able only to carry the weight of twenty-four hours—one day at a time. Start a new life each day.

When you mentally bring in regrets of the past or fears of the future, these are baggage you are not supposed to carry.

Bury them.

Don't carry them.

Face today with hope and courage.

You are learning to build your life one day at a time under My guidance. I am the architect and you are building as best as you can. I'm pleased with you.

Put away old mistakes of the past and start each day anew. I offer you a fresh start.

Forget about the future.
Live one day at a time.
All you really have is now.
Yesterday is gone.
Forget it.
Tomorrow never comes.
Don't worry.
All you have is the present.
Today is here.

231

When tomorrow comes, it is today.

Live today!

೦ᘓৎೲ

"Therefore do not worry about tomorrow, for tomorrow will worry about its own things. Sufficient for the day is its own trouble."
—Matthew 6:34 NKJV

REFLECTION:

ONLY LIVE IN THE PRESENT

చికిర

I only walk with you in the present, not in the future. Quit thinking about the future and wanting better things. I'm here with you in the present.

Start each day by asking Me for the strength to do My Will. Take each day and follow every good leading of your conscience. Don't look back.

Live now, in *the now*—the present. The past is gone, over with. You don't know what the future holds.

Live in the present—today. Forget the past unless there is one area of your life where you need to make amends with someone. If you need to make amends, do it, and then move on.

Cast off the past.

Press forward in faith, one day, one hour at a time.

Only live in the now.

చికిర

"When Jesus had raised Himself up and saw no one but the woman, He said to her, 'Woman, where are those accusers of yours? Has no one condemned you?' "She said, "No one, Lord.' "And Jesus said to her, "Neither do I condemn you; go and sin no more.'"

—Jesus, speaking to a woman caught in adultery, John 8:10-11 NKJV

"For God has not given us a spirit of fear, but of power and of love and of a sound mind."
—2 Timothy 1:7 NKJV

"Therefore, there is now no condemnation for those who are in Christ Jesus, because through Christ Jesus the law of the Spirit who gives life has set you free from the law of sin and death."—Romans 8:1-2

REFLECTION:

OUTCOMES

൞

Leave the outcome and timing up to Me. Give Me troubling or excitable situations—every situation—and ask for My Will to be done.

Because you are human, you will try to take it back, but give it to Me again and say "Thy Will be done." You might have to do this fifty times a day! But that's OK.

Watch Me work it out in My timing and according to My Will, which is always best.

൞

"Trust in the LORD with all your heart and lean not on your own understanding; in all your ways submit to him, and he will make your paths straight."—Proverbs 3:5-6

REFLECTION:

OVERCOME YOURSELF

⳩

Isn't it wonderful to discover that you are not the center of the universe?

You are one of my children, and you can depend on Me to guide you and give you strength. Your life is about loving Me and loving others. I'm glad you have taken yourself off the throne.

I will give you wisdom to take care of yourself. I'm behind you when you do the right thing.

Keep working to overcome your self-centeredness and selfish desire. Every time you overcome by trusting and obeying Me, I am glorified.

⳩

"He who is slow to anger is better than the mighty, And he who rules his spirit than he who takes a city." —Proverbs 16:32 NKJV

REFLECTION:

OVERWHELMED

⁂

You can get overwhelmed with all the different facets of your life:

- Family
- Job
- To-Do Lists
- Friends
- Hobbies
- Exercise
- Appointments
- Duties
- And more.

Get your focus back on Me. Give Me each one, one by one, and ask, "Thy Will be done." I will make your path straight.

⁂

"Cast all your anxiety on him because he cares for you." —1 Peter 5:7

"I instruct you in the way of wisdom and lead you along straight paths." —Proverbs 4:11

REFLECTION:

PAIN

CR8O

Pain is part of your spiritual growth.
Pain is a part of life.
Sometimes you just have to live through it.

Be transparent with Me and I will see you through. Don't hide your hurts from Me. Tell Me everything because I know it any way.

Hold My hand and I will lead you back to peace and joy after this storm. The sun will shine in your life again.

You can face all things through My power which strengthens you. You are deeply secure no matter what you are facing, because you have Me.

Try to remember that you are not the only one experiencing pain.

You will win.
Don't give up.

CR8O

"I am in pain and distress; may your salvation, O God, protect me." —Psalm 69:29.

"I can do all this through him who gives me strength." —Philippians 4:19

"For it is commendable if a man bears up under the pain of unjust suffering because he is conscious of God." —1 Peter 2:19

REFLECTION:

THE PAST

⊂ॐ⊃

Learning from the past is good.
Dwelling on the past is not good.

I am in the present, right now, with you. The next twenty-fours are all I want you to live. Live in the present—not in regrets of the past or fear of the future.

⊂ॐ⊃

"Forget the former things; do not dwell on the past. See, I am doing a new thing! Now it springs up; do you not perceive it? I am making a way in the desert and streams in the wasteland."—Isaiah 43:18-19

REFLECTION:

PEACE

☙❧

If you live the way I want you to live, you will have peace. Your soul will be calm. When your soul is calm, true spiritual work can be done in your mind, emotions, will, and body to give you strength to conquer and bear all things.

Peace is the result of righteousness.
There is no peace in wrongdoing.
Peace is the inheritance I have left you.

☙❧

"Peace I leave with you; my peace I give you. I do not give to you as the world gives. Do not let your hearts be troubled and do not be afraid." —John 14:27

☙❧

The result of peace will be a quiet, confident trust in Me. I want you to dwell in safety and in a quiet resting place.

You are learning how important peace is and not to move in any direction until you have My peace in your heart and mind.

CƷ℥Ɔ

"Depart from evil and do good; seek peace and pursue it." —Psalm 34:14

"Now may the Lord of peace himself give you peace at all times and in every way. The Lord be with all of you." —2 Thessalonians 3:16

"You will keep in perfect peace those whose minds are steadfast, because they trust in you." —Isaiah 26:3

"May the God of peace, who through the blood of the eternal covenant brought back from the dead our Lord Jesus, that great Shepherd of the sheep, equip you with everything good for doing his will, and may he work in us what is pleasing to him, through Jesus Christ, to whom be glory for ever and ever. Amen." —Hebrews 13:20-21

REFLECTION:

PEACE II

⊙৪৩

You are learning how important peace is and not to move in any direction until you have My peace in your heart and mind. You will find in Me a peace, a rest, a satisfaction that you won't find anywhere else. The world can't take it away. My presence will give you peace and My peace will wash all the irritants away. Now. . .

- Relax.
- Let My Spirit flow through you.
- Complete surrender of your life is the foundation of peace.
- Stay clear of storms or unpleasant change. Keep your life calm and unruffled.
- Keep free from disquieting or oppressive thoughts or emotions.
- Keep harmony in personal relations.
- Don't harbor disturbing thoughts.

Take care about these things and you will find peace.

⊙৪৩

"And let the peace (soul harmony which comes) from Christ rule (act as umpire

245

continually) in your hearts [deciding and set-tling with finality all questions that arise in your minds, in that peaceful state] to which as [members of Christ's] one body you were also called [to live]. And be thankful (appreciative), [giving praise to God always]."
—Colossians 3:15 AMP

"Now may the Lord of peace himself give you peace at all times and in every way. The Lord be with all of you." —2 Thessalonians 3:16

REFLECTION:

PEACE OF MIND

Surrendering to My Will is the way to peace of mind. Peace of mind is priceless.

You are finding more peace and contentment as you surrender to My Will. Life is falling into place like pieces of a puzzle. Confusion will no longer be predominant because you are finding your way.

You weren't meant to live in quiet desperation with fear and worries looming over every situation. Faith takes the power from fear and worry and then brings peace.

". . . Godliness with contentment is great gain." —1 Timothy 6:6

"Finally, brethren, farewell (rejoice)! Be strengthened (perfected, completed, made what you ought to be); be encouraged and consoled and comforted; be of the same [agreeable] mind one with another; live in peace, and [then] the God of love [Who is the Source of affection, goodwill, love, and benevolence toward men] and the Author

and Promoter of peace will be with you."
—2 Corinthians 13:11 AMP

REFLECTION:

PEOPLE PLEASING

C*380

When you fear displeasing people or you want people to like you, you become in bondage to them and then your thoughts become fixed on them.

To refocus your thoughts on Me, start saying My name.
Spend time alone with Me.

It doesn't matter what people think of you. You can do nothing about that. All that matters is what you think of them. Stop giving them free rent in your head.

C*380

". . . Behold, to obey is better than sacrifice . . ." 1 Samuel 15:22

"And whatever you do, whether in word or deed, do it all in the name of the Lord Jesus, giving thanks to God the Father through him." —Colossians 3:17

"But the LORD *said to Samuel, 'Do not consider his appearance or his height, for I have rejected him. The* LORD *does not look at*

the things people look at. People look at the outward appearance, but the Lord looks at the heart.'" —1 Samuel 16:7

"What, then, shall we say in response to these things? If God is for us, who can be against us? He who did not spare his own Son, but gave him up for us all—how will he not also, along with him, graciously give us all things? Who will bring any charge against those whom God has chosen? It is God who justifies. Who then is the one who condemns? No one. Christ Jesus who died—more than that, who was raised to life—is at the right hand of God and is also interceding for us. Who shall separate us from the love of Christ? Shall trouble or hardship or persecution or famine or nakedness or danger or sword?".
. . . No, in all these things we are more than conquerors through him who loved us.
—Romans 8:31-35

REFLECTION:

PERFECTIONISM

CℬℰO

You are learning that perfectionism stems from false pride.

I want you to be content with making progress, going forward, and growing.

Be willing to make mistakes and own up to them. You are on your way, making progress, and that's what's important.

If you stumble, stumble forward and keep going. You are becoming, and that's what's important. You won't ever arrive, but you are getting better and better every day—and that is what matters.

CℬℰO

"Pride goes before destruction, a haughty spirit before a fall." —Proverbs 16:18

"For everything in the world—the lust of the flesh, the lust of the eyes, and the pride of life—comes not from the Father but from the world. The world and its desires pass away, but whoever does the will of God lives forever." —1 John 2:16-17

REFLECTION:

Playing Ball

⋘⋙

When you watch children playing ball and some are serious players, giving their very best with each play, you feel pride at their giving it their all.

Now I am proud of the way you have played the balls that have come your way in life. I'm watching you and I'm pleased.

⋘⋙

"Now if you obey me fully and keep my covenant, then out of all nations you will be my treasured possession." —Exodus 19:5

REFLECTION:

PLANS

CԅՑՀO

I am planning for you. My ways are wonderful and beyond your knowledge.

My leading is entering your consciousness more and more, and it will bring you even more peace and joy.

There is beauty in a life guided by Me.
There is security in the feeling of being led by Me.

The consciousness of My guidance and the peace it brings is worth more than silver or gold, or any material thing.

CԅՑՀO

"For I know the plans I have for you," declares the LORD, "plans to prosper you and not to harm you, plans to give you hope and a future." —Jeremiah 29:11

REFLECTION:

POWER

⊂ЗଔⲞ

Link your frail nature with My strong, limitless
divine power.
When you are weak, I can be strong. There is no shame
in weakness.
Call on Me.
Think of Me and call on Me when you need to flee
temptation.
My power is your rescue lifeline.
My power is available to you to help you do the right thing.
Accept My power.

⊂ЗଔⲞ

*"He gives strength to the weary and increases
the power of the weak."* —Isaiah 40:29

REFLECTION:

Prayer I

Prayer is talking to Me.

A prayer of faith is a prayer of trust. As your faith rises to meet Me, you will feel My presence. You can be sure of some response from Me. I am pleased by your faith.

Be thankful for My grace and mercy, which are keeping you on the right path.

Faith, trust, and gratitude will bless you.

Don't get discouraged. I am pleased with your progress.

Just be honest with Me.

Tell Me you need Me.

Tell Me you are weak and afraid.

Tell Me what worries you.

Give it to Me and ask for My Will to be done.

Give it to Me and let go.

Watch Me work it out in My timing.

Trust Me with the outcome.

Pray for strength and that My Will be done.

Pray that you will have a listening ear so that I may speak to you.

Pray that you may have a waiting heart so that I may come to you.

"When I called, you answered me; you made me bold and stouthearted." —Psalm 138:3

"Do not be anxious about anything, but in every situation, by prayer and petition, with thanksgiving, present your requests to God." —Philippians 4:6

REFLECTION:

PRAYER II

Prayer is talking to Me. I already know your needs but prayer shows your need for Me.

I want you to talk to Me about everything. I desire to hear truth from your inner being.

Stay in constant communication with Me.

Seek no credit for the results of what you do. Pray that you may leave the outcome of your actions to Me.

Prayer is linking yourself to My mind and My Will.

Pray that I, God, will help you to become all that I would have you to be.

". . .Your Father knows what you need before you ask him." — Matthew 6:8

"Surely you desire truth in the inner parts; you teach me wisdom in the inmost place." —Psalm 51:6

". . . Pray continually. . ." — 1 Thessalonians 5:17

REFLECTION:

Prayer III

☙

Lord, you have given me a new life and I haven't done
one thing to deserve it.
I am so grateful to you!
Help me to serve others and give away what you have
so freely given me.
I pray I will seek no credit for the results of what I do.
I pray that I may leave the outcome of my actions
to You, God.
I love you.

You've been sent out by Me every morning to do My
Will. In the evening come back to Me and tell Me in quiet
communion that the message has been delivered or the
task done.

Prayer is the linking up of your spirit, soul, and mind to
Me, God. It can be a glance of faith, a grateful thought of My
goodness, a thought of My presence, or a feeling of security
knowing you are in My hands.

In gratitude and humility, turn to Me. Pray that you may
see the working of My Will in your life, and pray that you
may be content with whatever My Will is.

☙❧

"Be joyful in hope, patient in affliction, faithful in prayer." —Romans 12:12

REFLECTION:

PRIDE

ᲝᲖᲜᲔ

Your attitude toward life is changing from one of selfishness and pride to one of humility and gratitude. I enjoy your gratitude.

Pride comes before a fall, without exception.

The opposite of pride is humility. You learn humility through your failures.

I give My grace to the humble. You've done nothing to deserve My grace. It's a gift because of My love for you. I'm so glad you have found this gift.

ᲝᲖᲜᲔ

"Likewise you younger people, submit yourselves to your elders. Yes, all of you be submissive to one another, and be clothed with humility, for 'God resists the proud, But gives grace to the humble.'" —1 Peter 5:5 NKJV

"Where there is strife, there is pride, but wisdom is found in those who take advice." —Proverbs 13:10

"Pride goes before destruction, a haughty spirit before a fall." —Proverbs 16:18

"He went on: 'What comes out of a person is what defiles them. For it is from within, out of a person's heart, that evil thoughts come— sexual immorality, theft, murder, adultery, greed, malice, deceit, lewdness, envy, slander, arrogance and folly. All these evils come from inside and defile a person.'" —Mark 7:20-23

"I am the Lord; that is My name! And My glory I will not give to another, nor My praise to graven images." —Isaiah 42:8 AMP

REFLECTION:

Problems

ೞ

Some things you are totally powerless over. When you can't do anything about it yourself, put the whole problem in My hands. Turn it over to Me.

I am the power greater than you. Have nothing to do with it except to trust Me to take care of it for you.

Let the worry and fear go.
Let peace, joy, and contentment take their place.

Face the day's problems with Me and ask My help and guidance as to what you should do in every situation that may arise.

You can make use of your problems in helping other people. Your problems give you sympathy and understanding for others' problems. Unless you have been through the same experience, it's difficult to fully sympathize with what others are going through.

ೞ

"Rejoice in the Lord always. I will say it again: Rejoice! Let your gentleness be evident to all. The Lord is near. Do not be anxious about anything, but in every situation,

by prayer and petition, with thanksgiving, present your requests to God. And the peace of God, which transcends all understanding, will guard your hearts and your minds in Christ Jesus." —Philippians 4:4-7

"Therefore I tell you, do not worry about your life, what you will eat or drink; or about your body, what you will wear. Is not life more than food, and the body more than clothes? Look at the birds of the air; they do not sow or reap or store away in barns, and yet your heavenly Father feeds them. Are you not much more valuable than they? Can any one of you by worrying add a single hour to your life?

"And why do you worry about clothes? See how the flowers of the field grow. They do not labor or spin. Yet I tell you that not even Solomon in all his splendor was dressed like one of these. If that is how God clothes the grass of the field, which is here today and tomorrow is thrown into the fire, will he not much more clothe you—you of little faith? So do not worry, saying, 'What shall we eat?' or 'What shall we drink?' or 'What shall we wear?' For the pagans run after all these things, and your heavenly Father knows that

you need them. But seek first his kingdom and his righteousness, and all these things will be given to you as well. Therefore do not worry about tomorrow, for tomorrow will worry about itself. Each day has enough trouble of its own." —Matthew 6:25-34

"Each of you should use whatever gift you have received to serve others, as faithful stewards of God's grace in its various forms. If anyone speaks, they should do so as one who speaks the very words of God. If anyone serves, they should do so with the strength God provides, so that in all things God may be praised through Jesus Christ. To him be the glory and the power for ever and ever. Amen." —1 Peter 4:10-11

"Humble yourselves, therefore, under God's mighty hand, that he may lift you up in due time. Cast all your anxiety on him because he cares for you." —1 Peter 5:6-7

REFLECTION:

PROGRESS

Spiritual progress is what's important.

See around all the beauty and good in the world and you will see Me. Build on this each twenty-four hours.

Today, be more loving and unselfish than you were the day before.

You are a part of the good in the world. I'm pleased with you.

"Not that I have already obtained all this, or have already arrived at my goal, but I press on to take hold of that for which Christ Jesus took hold of me. Brothers and sisters, I do not consider myself yet to have taken hold of it. But one thing I do: Forgetting what is behind and straining toward what is ahead, I press on toward the goal to win the prize for which God has called me heavenward in Christ Jesus." —Philippians 3:12-14

"And we all, who with unveiled faces contemplate the Lord's glory, are being transformed into his image with ever-increasing

267

glory, which comes from the Lord, who is the Spirit." —2 Corinthians 3:18

REFLECTION:

PROTECTION

CREO

I will protect you from the forces of evil if you will rely on Me. Once you have surrendered your life to Me and trust Me, you have My stamp of approval, which is My Holy Spirit, and all My strength will protect you.

My help is always ready and available to you so you can face anything. You can rely on Me and feel deeply secure no matter what happens to you.

Never doubt that My Spirit is with you, always, wherever you are, to keep you on the right path.

- Believe in My nearness and My availability.
- Seek the security of My shelter during a storm.
- Fear, worry, and doubt are disloyalty to Me. Trust Me completely.
- Practice saying, "Everything will be okay." Say it until you feel it deeply.

CREO

"You are my hiding place; you will protect me from trouble and surround me with songs of deliverance." —Psalm 32:7

"Keep and protect me, O God, for in You I have found refuge, and in You do I put my trust and hide myself.—Psalm 16:1 AMP

"Vindicate me, O Lord, for I have walked in my integrity; I have [expectantly] trusted in, leaned on, and relied on the Lord without wavering and I shall not slide."
—Psalm 26:5 AMP

REFLECTION:

PURPOSE

☙❧

Reprogramming your soul—your mind, your will, and your emotions—is what life is about.

People mostly choose what's good for the body, but I want you to make reprogramming your soul a priority. Then choose what's best for your body. A wonderful molding of your character will take place.

Choose good in the choices you make each day.

As you do this, the purpose of your life will be accomplished and I will be glorified.

Live for a purpose greater than yourself.

Glorify Me in your love and service to others.

☙❧

"Now the mind of the flesh [which is sense and reason without the Holy Spirit] is death [death that comprises all the miseries arising from sin, both here and hereafter]. But the mind of the [Holy] Spirit is life and [soul] peace [both now and forever]."
—Romans 8:6 AMP

"For who has known or understood the mind (the counsels and purposes) of the Lord so

as to guide and instruct Him and give Him knowledge? But we have the mind of Christ (the Messiah) and do hold the thoughts (feelings and purposes) of His heart."
—1 Corinthians 2:16 AMP

"By this all men will know that you are my disciples, if you love one another."—John 13:35

"Do not conform to the pattern of this world, but be transformed by the renewing of your mind. Then you will be able to test and approve what God's will is—his good, pleasing and perfect will."—Romans 12:2

REFLECTION:

Quiet Times with Me

CℜEO

I'm waiting for you.

When you spend this quiet time with Me on a regular
basis it builds your faith.

It strengthens our relationship.

It gives you strength to handle each day.

It reminds you that I'm with you to help you.

I can give you all the help you need.

The major purpose of our time together is waiting
for divine guidance from Me after your prayer and our
communication.

As you spend quiet time with Me and you are in My
presence, I will transform you mentally and spiritually. Your
greatest spiritual growth occurs during this time spent with
Me each day.

Each morning have a quiet time with Me and ask Me for
the power to stay in My presence for the next twenty-four
hours. Each night thank Me for helping you.

Let your spirit touch My Spirit. This is the time to do it.
Sense My presence.

We have tender intimacies together in our quiet communion times.

CℜEO

"You make known to me the path of life;
you will fill me with joy in your presence,
with eternal pleasures at your right hand."
—Psalm: 16:11

"Look to the LORD and his strength; seek his
face always." —1 Chronicles 16:11

"One thing I ask from the LORD, this only do I
seek: that I may dwell in the house of the LORD
all the days of my life, to gaze on the beauty of
the LORD and to seek him in his temple. . . . My
heart says of you, 'Seek his face!" Your face,
LORD, I will seek.'" —Psalm: 27:4, 8

REFLECTION:

REJECTION

⚮

Rejection from others hurts you until you realize this:
It doesn't matter what others think of you. You can't
do anything about it.

All that matters is what you think of them.

That's what matters.

⚮

"Who shall bring any charge against God's elect [when it is] God Who justifies [that is, Who puts us in right relation to Himself? Who shall come forward and accuse or impeach those whom God has chosen? Will God, Who acquits us?] Who is there to condemn [us]? Will Christ Jesus (the Messiah), Who died, or rather Who was raised from the dead, Who is at the right hand of God actually pleading as He intercedes for us?"
—Romans 8:33-34 AMP

REFLECTION:

RELATIONSHIPS

ⳄⳄ

Follow My guidance in all personal relationships. This is a spiritual thing and you can't rely on your own wisdom. Be guided by Me in human relationships if you accomplish anything of value.

Don't weaken your spiritual power by letting people upset you. If you feel slighted, your pride gets ruffled, don't let these feelings in. You will lose your peace. Is it worth it?

Don't let anyone provoke you. It's not worth losing your peace.

ⳄⳄ

"Turn from evil and do good; seek peace and pursue it." — Psalm 34:14

". . . Whoever would love life and see good days must keep their tongue from evil and their lips from deceitful speech. They must turn from evil and do good; they must seek peace and pursue it." — 1 Peter 3:10-11

REFLECTION:

REPENT

൭ൠ

Repentance isn't "doing" something about your sin; rather it means admitting you "can't do" anything about your sin. You need Me to free you from what you have done or what has a hold on you. I've got the power to do this. You don't.

True repentance is a powerful thing because it is *a gift* from Me. It has nothing to do with "striving" or "trying" or "will power." True repentance is total trust in My mercy and grace to free you and cleanse you from your sin.

Come to Me and give up! Don't rely on holding onto anything! Be transparent with Me and trust Me. Depend totally on My mercy and grace. I love you! I am committed to you to take care of you because I love you beyond your understanding, but you don't spend time with Me in heartfelt communion. When you truly love someone, you spend time with them.

Love equals quality time spent together.
I'm waiting for you.

൭ൠ

"But I have this [one charge to make] against
you: that you have left (abandoned) the love

that you had at first [you have deserted Me, your first love]. Remember then from what heights you have fallen. Repent (change the inner man to meet God's will) and do the works you did previously [when first you knew the Lord], or else I will visit you and remove your lampstand from its place, unless you change your mind and repent." —Revelation 2:4-5

"In those days there appeared John the Baptist, preaching in the Wilderness (Desert) of Judea and saying, Repent (think differently; change your mind, regretting your sins and changing your conduct), for the kingdom of heaven is at hand." —Matthew 3:1-2 AMP

REFLECTION:

RESENTMENT AND BITTERNESS

⊂ℬ⊃

Lose resentment.

Lose bitterness.

Resentment is when you continue to refeed something. Wanting people to pay for what they have done only causes you to be frustrated and feel bitter. Resentment and bitterness only punish you. They don't affect your enemies. They destroy your peace and they hurt you more than they hurt others.

Resentment and bitterness are like poison in your system.

Stay in communion with Me and I will help you get rid of this poison.

Resentment will only lead you to unhappiness.

Don't let people live rent free in your head.

⊂ℬ⊃

"See to it that no one falls short of the grace of God and that no bitter root grows up to cause trouble and defile many." —Hebrews 12:15

"Get rid of all bitterness, rage and anger, brawling and slander, along with every form of malice." —Ephesians 4:31

"Resentment kills a fool, and envy slays the simple." —Job 5:2

REFLECTION:

Rest

Come to Me and I will give you rest.

- Rest and peace are partners and you will find them in Me.
- Rest will refresh your soul.
- Rest relieves you from worry and fear and gives you emotional calm.

Your soul has found its home of rest in Me, and now your real life has begun. You can only do good work when you are calm and at rest. Emotional upsets make you useless.

I am your refuge, your place of rest. I'll hold you in My arms when you come to Me. You can lay down your burdens and get some rest. Nothing can seriously upset you or make you afraid if I am truly your refuge.

I will shelter you, love you, and protect you. You will find rest when you come to Me and know of My grace and love for you.

I am your support and your safety.
Rely on My Will and purposes for your life.
Relax in My arms.
They will support you.

 CREO

"Come to me, all you who are weary and burdened, and I will give you rest. Take my yoke upon you and learn from me, for I am gentle and humble in heart, and you will find rest for your souls. For my yoke is easy and my burden is light." —Matthew 11:28-30 AMP

REFLECTION:

REWARDS

☙

You are getting better at not seeking people's approval and desiring the world's applause.

There is one reward spoken that is greater than any wealth or world fame and recognition. They are My quiet, private words to you: *"Well done, My good and faithful servant."*

You have become content leading a simple life, listening for My voice and following Me.

☙

The LORD is my shepherd, I shall not be in want. He makes me lie down in green pastures, he leads me beside quiet waters, he restores my soul. He guides me in paths of righteousness for his name's sake. . .

—Psalm 23:1-3

"My sheep listen to my voice; I know them, and they follow me." —John 10:27

"Whether you turn to the right or to the left, your ears will hear a voice behind you, saying, 'This is the way; walk in it.'" —Isaiah 30:21

REFLECTION:

RIGHTS

Continually ask for one thing:

"Thy Will" not "my will" be done. This is the key to
abundant life.
My power can accomplish My Will.

Modern culture teaches you to fight for your rights, push your way to the top, and "look out for number one."

"Thy Will be done" is the approach to life that has the foundation of faith. It will give you peace and joy, and it will honor Me.

"For we are God's handiwork, created in Christ Jesus to do good works, which God prepared in advance for us to do. . . . Consequently, you are no longer foreigners and strangers, but fellow citizens with God's people and also members of his household, built on the foundation of the apostles and prophets, with Christ Jesus himself as the chief cornerstone." —Ephesians 2:10, 19-20

"Your attitude should be the same as that of Christ Jesus . . ."—Phlippians 2:5

REFLECTION:

SATISFACTION

੭੩੪

There is only one way to get satisfaction out of life and that is to live the way I want you to. I will show you the way. Trust Me.

Think of the eternal value in the work you do. This gives the world meaning to you.

You have a place in this world and you count.

> *"You did not choose me, but I chose you and appointed you so that you might go and bear fruit—fruit that will last—and so that whatever you ask in my name the Father will give you."* —John 15:16

> *"For he chose us in him before the creation of the world to be holy and blameless in his sight."* —Ephesians 1:4

REFLECTION:

SEASHELLS IN THE SAND

༺✦༻

As you walk behind precious barefoot children in their little swimsuits, full of delight as they find small shells in the sand along the shoreline, seeing their joy warms your heart. They are enjoying such a simple thing in life.

Your heart bursts with love when they are your own, in your earthly family.

I am looking at you like you are looking them.
That's how much I love you.

༺✦༻

"No, the Father himself loves you because you have loved me and have believed that I came from God." —John 16:27

REFLECTION:

SECURITY

༺༺

I will supply all your needs.

At times you have different needs and I am your security.

When you are weak I will give you strength.

When you are strong I will give you My tenderness.

When you are tempted and fall, I'll give you My saving grace.

When you are lonely, I'll be your friend.

You need Me and I'm here for you.

Nothing should seriously upset you because you have a deep, abiding faith that I will take care of you. Don't get upset about the surface wrongness of things, but feel deeply secure in Me.

I am your shelter—your security—and underneath everything are My everlasting arms. I am your loving protection.

I am your place to relax where you can lay down your burdens and get relief from the cares of life.

Meditate on these words until they sink into your soul: I am your security.

༺༺

"The eternal God is your refuge, and underneath are the everlasting arms. He will drive

291

out your enemy before you, saying, 'Destroy him!'" —Deuteronomy 33:27

"To him who is able to keep you from stumbling and to present you before his glorious presence without fault and with great joy—to the only God our Savior be glory, majesty, power and authority, through Jesus Christ our Lord, before all ages, now and forevermore! Amen." —Jude 24-25

"No temptation has overtaken you except what is common to mankind. And God is faithful; he will not let you be tempted beyond what you can bear. But when you are tempted, he will also provide a way out so that you can endure it." —1 Corinthians 10:13

"You, dear children, are from God and have overcome them, because the one who is in you is greater than the one who is in the world." —1 John 4:4

"My Father, who has given them to me, is greater than all; no one can snatch them out of my Father's hand." —John 10:29

REFLECTION:

SELF-CENTEREDNESS

ᘓᕲᕣ

You are becoming less sensitive to slights or insults.
You are becoming less sensitive to being "left out."

These are marks of maturity. When you are wrapped up in Me these things don't mean anything and you do not notice them as much.

Self-pity is childish. Don't give in to it. Laugh at it and move on. You have matured past this.

ᘓᕲᕣ

"That is why, for Christ's sake, I delight in weaknesses, in insults, in hardships, in persecutions, in difficulties. For when I am weak, then I am strong." —2 Corinthians 12:10

"Who is wise and understanding among you? Let them show it by their good life, by deeds done in the humility that comes from wisdom. But if you harbor bitter envy and selfish ambition in your hearts, do not boast about it or deny the truth. Such "wisdom" does not come downfrom heaven but is earthly, unspiritual, demonic." —James 3:13-15

"Do nothing out of selfish ambition or vain conceit. Rather, in humility value others above yourselves, not looking to your own interests but each of you to the interests of the others." —Philippians 2:3-4

". . . For it is from within, out of a person's heart, that evil thoughts come—sexual immorality, theft, murder, adultery, greed, malice, deceit, lewdness, envy, slander, arrogance and folly. All these evils come from inside and defile a person." —Mark 7:20-23

REFLECTION:

SELFISHNESS

CR80

It isn't the difficulties in life you have to conquer so much as it is your own selfishness.

When you are having a problem in a situation, check in with Me. Let's monitor your selfishness together. As you learn to overcome selfishness, every blow against it shapes your eternal life. This is good. You are gaining My power and strength.

You can't believe in Me and keep your selfish ways. The self shrivels up and dies and My life becomes larger in you. Your goal for life is the gradual elimination of your selfishness and the growth of your love for Me and other human beings.

You are taking on more and more the likeness of Me. Those who see you now see some of the power of God's grace at work in a human life.

Work at overcoming yourself, your selfish desires, and your self-centeredness. You will not ever accomplish these goals completely but your selfishness will diminish as you realize the universe does not revolve around you.

CR80

"Turn my heart toward your statutes and not toward selfish gain." —Psalm 119:36

"An unfriendly person pursues selfish ends and against all sound judgment starts quarrels."—Proverbs 18:1

"Do nothing out of selfish ambition or vain conceit. Rather, in humility value others above yourselves . . ."—Philippians 2:3

"Love is patient, love is kind. It does not envy, it does not boast, it is not proud. It does not dishonor others, it is not self-seeking, it is not easily angered, it keeps no record of wrongs."—1 Corinthians 13:4-5

REFLECTION:

SERVE

⚬⃝⚬

You are brought closer to Me as you serve others.

- Serve cheerfully without complaining.
- Think less about yourself and more about other people.

The first quality of greatness is service. Remember this: I am the greatest servant of all.

Be a channel for My life to be received by others.

Don't ever point out their weakness to other people. Share your own weaknesses, temptations, and sins, and they will find Me.

Try to understand others and what they have been through. You have probably been through similar trials yourself.

Serving Me gives full and complete satisfaction. Serving the world does not. You can't serve both or your life will be fragmented and full of confusion.

Your rewards are great for serving Me. Some of those rewards you will receive in this earthly world.

⚬⃝⚬

"For you, brethren, were [indeed] called to freedom; only [do not let your] freedom be an incentive to your flesh and an opportunity or excuse [for selfishness], but

298

through love you should serve one another."
—Galatians 5:13 AMP

"If I must boast, I will boast of the things that show my weakness."—2 Corinthians 11:30

REFLECTION:

Sex

⬥

I created sex. It is not to be despised or hated. It's never to be used selfishly or distorted.

Living close to Me puts sex in its proper place and gives you peace.

Sex is powerful. It can lead you astray when used selfishly. Then you are out of My Will and your peace will leave.

Your body is a gift from Me.

You are too valuable to let the wrong person open this gift. Temptation can be strong but let Me fight this battle for you. This wonderful gift houses your spirit and your soul. Don't give this gift to those who are not interested in either.

You are My precious treasure and I will protect you if you lean on Me. My Holy Spirit dwells within you with all you need to make right choices.

⬥

"You are not your own; you were bought at a price. Therefore honor God with your body." — 1 Corinthians 6: 20

"Dear friends, I urge you, as foreigners and exiles, to abstain from sinful desires, which wage war against your soul. Live such good lives among the pagans that, though they accuse you of doing wrong, they may see your good deeds and glorify God on the day he visits us." — 1 Peter 2:11-12

You are to abstain from food sacrificed to idols, from blood, from the meat of strangled animals and from sexual immorality. You will do well to avoid these things. — Acts 15:29

REFLECTION:

SHINE

෮෫෨

You are arising from your gloom and are My shining ambassador. Arise to this new life and let My glory shine through you. My glory shines in the beauty of your character.

You are a reflection of My divine light and life. Even though there is darkness on the earth, My glory has arisen upon you and shall be seen on you.

෮෫෨

"Arise, shine, for your light has come, and the glory of the LORD rises upon you. See, darkness covers the earth and thick darkness is over the peoples, but the LORD rises upon you and his glory appears over you."
—Isaiah 60:1-2

REFLECTION:

SIN

꩜

Don't be dependent on sin—get free from it.

Don't depend on sin to make you happy or to lift you up when you are low.

Sinning seems harmless at first but eventually the bad effects come more and more to outweigh the good. When you accept a bad habit into your life, you are also accepting the end result of that habit. Don't do it.

Run from sin.
I have an abundant life for you.

Do you remember the guilt you lived with? The low self-esteem? Always feeling others were better than you? Don't go there. Stay close to Me.

Remember this: Friendships in sin are based on selfishness. People use people for their own pleasure.

Real friendship is based on unselfishness and a desire to help each other.

꩜

"The thief comes only to steal and kill and destroy; I have come that they may have life, and have it to the full." —John 10:10

"Submit yourselves, then, to God. Resist the devil, and he will flee from you." —James 4:7

REFLECTION:

SITUATIONS

☙☙

Give Me each situation in your life.

Ask that My Will be done—not your will, not anyone else's will, but My Will be done.

Let go of it.

Give it to Me.

Leave the results to Me.

Leave the outcome to Me.

Leave the timing to Me.

Get out of the way.

Your human nature will try to take it back. Do the process all over again. Sometimes you might have to give Me something fifty times a day or more. That's okay. Just do it as many times as it takes.

☙☙

"Roll your works upon the Lord [commit and trust them wholly to Him; He will cause your thoughts to become agreeable to His will, and] so shall your plans be established and succeed." —Proverbs 16:3 AMP

REFLECTION:

SLEEPING CHILDREN

છ૩૪૦

You look at sleeping children and see them as precious,
magnificent creations. Their eyelashes are beautiful. Their
ears are cute. You look at their features and marvel at
their beauty.
As you snuggle in at bedtime, know that I am looking at
you like you are looking at them.
I love you.

છ૩૪૦

*"The Spirit himself testifies with our spirit
that we are God's children."* —Romans 8:16

*"When you lie down, you will not be afraid;
when you lie down, your sleep will be
sweet."* —Proverbs 3:24

REFLECTION:

STAY ON TRACK

CR80

Spiritual discipline of yourself is absolutely necessary before My power is given to you. All your life is a preparation for more good to come when I know you are ready for it. When you see My power manifested in others, it's because they have made themselves ready.

When you get off track, repent and come back to Me. That's all it takes. My strength is made perfect in your weakness.

CR80

"My flesh and my heart may fail, but God is the strength of my heart and my portion forever." —Psalm 73:26

"I know that you have little strength, yet you have kept my word and have not denied my name." —Revelation 3:8

"Stand therefore [hold your ground], having tightened the belt of truth around your loins and having put on the breastplate of integrity and of moral rectitudeand right standing with God. . ." —Ephesians 6:14 AMP

REFLECTION:

STRAYING

⊂ॐ∽

The cure for straying is to stay so close to Me that nothing, no other interest, can seriously come between you and Me.

Sure of that, you will stay close to My side just as a little lamb stays close to its mother. Knowing this, nothing can cause you to seriously stray from Me.

I've promised you peace if you stay close to Me. Comfort comes with peace, and both of these bring real inward happiness.

⊂ॐ∽

"What do you think? If a man owns a hundred sheep, and one of them wanders away, will he not leave the ninety-nine on the hills and go to look for the one that wandered off? And if he finds it, truly I tell you, he is happier about that one sheep than about the ninety-nine that did not wander off. In the same way your Father in heaven is not willing that any of these little ones should perish." —Matthew 18:12-14

"Come near to God and he will come near to you." —James 4:8

REFLECTION:

STRENGTH

CℬℰƆ

I will give you the necessary strength for each task today. Ask Me for the strength you need each day.

Face each challenge today and accept responsibility. For each challenge that comes your way today I will give you strength to face it. Don't hold back.

Always remember that you are weak *but I am strong*.

I know all about your weakness. I hear your every cry for mercy and every plea for help. I see every sign of weariness, every sorrow over failure, and every weakness you express.

When you are weak, then I am strong to help you. Trust Me enough and your weakness will not matter.

Through your own free will, ask Me for My strength. It is always available to you. You can't make too many demands on Me for strength. Remain close to Me and I will give you all the power and strength you need.

CℬℰƆ

"But he said to me, 'My grace is sufficient for you, for my power is made perfect in weakness." Therefore I will boast all the more

gladly about my weaknesses, so that Christ's power may rest on me.'" —2 Corinthians 12:9

REFLECTION:

STRENGTH II

ऒ३४ऒ

"I can do all things through Christ who strengthens me" does not mean "Do all things and rely on Me for strength." It means to do the things you believe I want you to do. Then you can rely on My strength.

When you are sure of My guidance, you can claim My strength. A servant begs, a child takes possession of. Don't beg, because My strength is for you to take. You are My child. You can claim My strength to meet every situation when you are on the right course.

Claim a new supply of strength constantly.
You have a right to claim it.
Use your right.

ऒ३४ऒ

"Now may the God of peace, who through the blood of the eternal covenant brought back from the dead our Lord Jesus, that great Shepherd of the sheep, equip you with everything good for doing his will, and may he work in us what is pleasing to him, through Jesus Christ, to whom be glory for ever and ever. Amen." —Hebrews 13:20-21

REFLECTION:

STRESS

⋘⋙

Don't bring into today what you might do tomorrow.

When you think constantly about what you need to do "tomorrow," rehearsing what you will do or say, you are in control. Being self-sufficient is not trusting Me. Trust Me enough to let things happen without striving and manipulating. I will work everything together for your good and my glory.

Get your eyes back on Me and you won't have stress. There is enough time in each twenty-four hours to do everything I've called you to do. Rest in Me as you surrender your will and say, "Thy Will be done."

You would like an uncluttered life and that is a fantasy. I want you to live above the circumstances with Me. Remember that I have called you and I will do it.

Accept each day as it comes and find Me in the midst of it. I won't ever leave you.

I love you.

⋘⋙

"For I know the plans I have for you,"
declares the LORD, "plans to prosper you and

not to harm you, plans to give you hope and a future." —Jeremiah 29:11

"He who calls you is faithful, who also will do it." —1 Thessalonians 5:24 NKJV

REFLECTION:

STRESS II

❧

Take your troubles as they come one by one and maintain calmness and composure amid pressing duties and unending engagements.

Rise above the circumstances by coming alone with Me. When you rise above, you have discovered a priceless secret of daily living. Even if you have some misfortune because of circumstances beyond your control, or some handicap, live each day with poise and peace of mind. If you do this, you have succeeded where most people fail.

❧

"Better a patient person than a warrior, one with self-control than one who takes a city." —Proverbs 16:32

"Like a city whose walls are broken through is a person who lacks self-control." —Proverbs 25:28

REFLECTION:

SUCCESS

☙❧

Your true measure of success is your spiritual progress. The day your body dies and you are in My presence you will know this for sure.

Others should be able to see this progress because it is a demonstration of My Will in your life. The measure of My Will worked out in your life is the true measure of success.

You are doing your best each day to demonstrate the power of My Will and your example is revealing My grace to the hearts of others.

☙❧

"He holds success in store for the upright, he is a shield to those whose walk is blameless."—Proverbs 2:7

REFLECTION:

SUFFERING

☙❧

Accept the difficulties and sufferings in life as an opportunity to relate with sympathy and understanding when others are suffering. Unless we have been through a similar circumstance we can't relate to others.

Everything that comes your way is part of life. Make use of it by helping others.

You can be thankful for comfort only if you have known the pain of suffering. You certainly have known that pain.

I am the God of all comfort.
Comforting is what I do.
Let Me comfort you.

☙❧

"Praise be to the God and Father of our Lord Jesus Christ, the Father of compassion and the God of all comfort, who comforts us in all our troubles, so that we can comfort those in any trouble with the comfort we ourselves receive from God." — 2 Corinthians 1:3-4

REFLECTION:

SUFFERING II

CREO

I never promised I would take you out of adversity,
But I've promised to go through it with you and be there
when you get through.
Just hold on to Me because I'm there with you.
Don't give in—just hold on.
This is progress.
I'm not looking for perfection.

CRED

"... we also glory in our sufferings, because
we know that suffering produces perseverance; perseverance, character; and character, hope." —Romans 5:3-4

"But how is it to your credit if you receive a
beating for doing wrong and endure it? But
if you suffer for doing good and you endure
it, this is commendable before God. To this
you were called, because Christ suffered
for you, leaving you an example, that you
should follow in his steps. 'He committed no
sin, and no deceit was found in his mouth.'
When they hurled their insults at him, he did

not retaliate; when he suffered, he made no threats. Instead, he entrusted himself to him who judges justly." — 1 Peter 2:20-23

REFLECTION:

SURRENDER

❦

As you grow closer to Me, your personality will change. Spiritual experience with Me changes one's personality. More often the changes will be gradual rather than sudden. Spending time with Me is the secret.

Surrendering your life and your will to Me will give you the abundant life I've promised.

The *length* of your surrendered life isn't what counts. It's the *quality* of your surrendered life that counts.

As you spend time with Me, you will undergo a profound alteration to your reaction to life. You can't do this on your own. Spending time with Me does it.

❦

". . . I have come that they may have life, and that they may have it more abundantly."
—John 10:10b NKJV

Therefore, I urge you, brothers and sisters, in view of God's mercy, to offer your bodies as a living sacrifice, holy and pleasing to God— this is your true and proper worship. Do not conform to the pattern of this world, but be transformed by the renewing of your mind.

325

Then you will be able to test and approve what God's will is—his good, pleasing and perfect will.—Romans 12:1-2

REFLECTION:

Surrender II

୧୨୫୭

To surrender is to put your life in My hands.

Letting go of everything and everybody is the secret to surrender. Ask Me to help you be willing to let go. Give everything and everybody to Me and don't try to keep one part for yourself.

Ask Me to remove every defect of character that stands in the way of our relationship and of being used for the benefit of others.

୧୨୫୭

"Have mercy on me, O God, according to your unfailing love; according to your great compassion blot out my transgressions. Wash away all my iniquity and cleanse me from my sin." —Psalm 51:1-2

"Incline your ear [submit and consent to the divine will] and come to Me; hear, and your soul will revive. . ." —Isaiah 55:3 AMP

"See if there is any offensive way in me, and lead me in the way everlasting."
—Psalm 139:24

REFLECTION

SUSTENANCE

❦

Your body needs food to sustain itself. Your soul needs sustaining, too. Trying to do My Will in your life is the nourishment for your soul. Your soul starves from failing to do My Will.

Partaking of My Will is spiritual food. It will give you strength and peace.

❦

"For the kingdom of God is not a matter of eating and drinking, but of righteousness, peace and joy in the Holy Spirit . . ."
—Romans 14:17

REFLECTION:

TEMPTATION

C380

Temptation will come.

- Get prepared for it by spending time with Me.
- Read the Bible and learn the forms it will take.
- When you recognize temptation, turn away quickly.
- Don't contemplate anything about it—see it for what it really is. It is destruction for you and for others.

When you accept something into your life, you are accepting the end result, whether you know it or not.

My strength is made perfect in weakness. If you fall into the temptation, come back to Me quickly. Don't wait.

Every time you resist the slightest temptation, you are honoring Me.

Don't fear temptation. I will give you what it takes to overcome. I will give you the strength to face it and overcome it.

C380

You can overcome any temptation with My Help.
Therefore, do not fear.

*"Your word I have hidden in my heart,
That I might not sin against You."*
—Psalm 119:11 NKJV

REFLECTION:

Thoughts

CR8O

Thoughts of Me will be like a balm for your fears and worries.

Praying to Me will help you find healing for hurt feelings and resentments and will soothe your soul.

Thinking of Me will cause doubts and fears to leave.
Faith and love will flow in and a peace will come that the world can't give or take away.
I will help you live.

Be on guard against wrong thinking. Making wrong choices always starts with thinking a wrong thought. Your subconscious has to be reeducated or reprogrammed. It used to be the case that before your feet hit the floor after sleeping, your mind used to have a negative thought. I want you to focus on hope and love now.

Trust and love are the solvents to apply to negative thinking.

- Worry and negative thoughts will fade away.
- Trust and love will protect your thinking. This reprogramming will happen a little at a time—but it can be done.

കൃൻ

"Do not be anxious about anything, but in every situation, by prayer and petition, with thanksgiving, present your requests to God. And the peace of God, which transcends all understanding, will guard your hearts and your minds in Christ Jesus. Finally, brothers and sisters, whatever is true, whatever is noble, whatever is right, whatever is pure, whatever is lovely, whatever is admirable—if anything is excellent or praiseworthy—think about such things." —Philippians 4:6-8

REFLECTION:

THOUGHTS II

∽◌∾

Do you remember when you wanted a life of excitement and extravagant material things? You have to re-educate your mind with My strength and wisdom and build a new way of looking at things.

Strive to live a decent, honest, unselfish life.

- Peace is priceless.
- Joy is priceless.
- Faith is priceless.
- Family and friends are priceless.
- My free gift of life is priceless.
- The air you breathe is priceless.
- The sun, moon, and stars are priceless.

Set your deepest affections on spiritual things and not material things. Set your mind on things that will help your spiritual growth, not hinder it. Being at one with Me is the highest aspiration you can have.

Change your way of thinking.

- Give up resentments.
- Stop being too sensitive and too easily hurt.
- Refuse to be selfish.
- Keep your thoughts on Me and meditate on the way I want you to live.
- Train your mind in quiet communion with Me.

You can't be assured of spiritual things with your intellect. Spiritual things are confirmed in your heart. Think of Me more with your heart than with your head. Open your heart by faith to Me.

∞

"I rejoice in following your statutes as one rejoices in great riches. I meditate on your precepts and consider your ways. I delight in your decrees; I will not neglect your word."—Psalm 119:14-16

REFLECTION:

THY WILL BE DONE

❧

Make a union between My purposes and your purposes by saying the most powerful four words to Me: "Thy Will be done."

When we have a oneness of purpose between us, we are in harmony and you will have harmony with others. Good will come, because you have gotten into the stream of goodness.

Pray like this: "May Your Will be done in and through me today."

When you trust Me to this extent, your whole body will be full of light. The eye of your soul is your will. When you trust Me to say "Thy Will be done" today, your soul will be full of light.

❧

"The eye is the lamp of the body. If your eyes are healthy, your whole body will be full of light." —Matthew 6:22

"Your eye is the lamp of your body. When your eyes are healthy, your whole body also is full

of light. But when they are unhealthy, your body also is full of darkness." —Luke 11:34

REFLECTION:

TIMING

⋇

There is a proper time for everything. Learn not to do things at the wrong time, before you are ready or before the conditions are right.

It's tempting to do things quickly instead of waiting for the proper time. Time is important.

Learn in the little daily situations of life to delay action until you are sure you are doing the right thing at the right time.

Do not be like the many who lack balance and timing in their lives.

⋇

"There is a time for everything, and a season for every activity under the heavens."
—Ecclesiastes 3:1

REFLECTION:

TRUST

Some things may not always seem the best at the present time, but you cannot see as far ahead as I can. I will work everything out for good because I love you and you love Me.

I have called you. I have destined you to be formed into the image of My son.

When you trust in a crutch, you cannot learn from Me. The crutch needs to be discarded with a willingness to walk in My power and Spirit. My power will so invigorate you that you will walk in victory. You will walk with Me step by step, one day at a time.

If you believe that I saved you, then you must believe I'm going to continue to save you and keep you in the way that you should go. Even a human rescuer would not save you from drowning and throw you back into deep and dangerous waters. No! The rescuer would place you in a dry place to restore you.

I am your Rescuer.
I will do this and even more.
I will not throw you overboard if you are depending on Me.

"Trust in the L*ORD* *with all your heart and lean not on your own understanding; in all your ways submit to him, and he will make your paths straight."* —Proverbs 3:5-6

REFLECTION:

TRUST II

⁂

When you cry out for Me to help you with your unbelief, it's your heart expressing its frailty. It signifies your sincere desire for progress.

Just fall into absolute trust in Me. Your cry is heard, and I honor it.

Trust Me enough and your weakness will not matter.

⁂

"In the same way, the Spirit helps us in our weakness. We do not know what we ought to pray for, but the Spirit himself intercedes for us through wordless groans." —Romans 8:26

⁂

PRAYER:

Dear God, I put my life and all decisions in Your hands, just as a small child places a tangled chain or tangled string in the hands of a loving mother to untangle.

I love you and trust you.

REFLECTION:

Unanswered Questions

⋙⋘

There will be unanswered questions that you may never solve until you get to heaven—questions about suffering, the loss of loved ones, why people are maimed and deformed, questions about evil. Many seemingly unanswerable questions. . .

Don't fret over these, because you can't solve them. Live your life one day at a time, one chapter at a time, giving Me each day with your will and asking for My Will to be done.

Keep going forward and not backward.

⋙⋘

"'For my thoughts are not your thoughts, neither are your ways my ways,' declares the Lord. 'As the heavens are higher than the earth, so are my ways higher than your ways and my thoughts than your thoughts.'"
—Isaiah 55:8-9

REFLECTION:

WAITING

⊂ॐ⊃

Waiting is difficult, more difficult than hard work, but necessary.

There is a time for everything. Learn to wait patiently until the right time comes.

Don't go on what you see, because I am working in the background.

Have faith that My Will shall be done.

Wait with patience. Your life is a preparation for something better to come because you are doing what's right. I have a plan for your life and this plan will work out in time.

When you don't know what to do, wait until I open the way for you. Waiting is hard. Trust is the key. Read Scriptures about hope, and then wait.

⊂ॐ⊃

"Even youths grow tired and weary, and young men stumble and fall; but those who hope in the LORD will renew their strength. They will soar on wings like eagles; they will run and not grow weary, they will walk and not be faint." —Isaiah 40:31

REFLECTION:

WAITING II

☙❧

Rely on Me.
Trust Me to the limit.
Wait on Me until I show you My Will.
Wait and trust and hope until I show you the way.
Wait for guidance for each important decision.
Meet the test of waiting until a thing seems right before you do it.
My guidance will come. Wait for it.
Your human activity can inflict harm to My plan and hinder spiritual growth.
Wait patiently for My Will to be revealed.
The right outcome will be accomplished at the right time.
Be led by your inner consciousness of Me.
You can't rush an answer to prayer.

☙❧

"Wait on the LORD; Be of good courage, And He shall strengthen your heart; Wait, I say, on the Lord!" —Psalm 27:14 AMP

"My soul, wait only upon God and silently submit to Him; for my hope and expectation are from Him." —Psalm 62:5

REFLECTION:

WALKING WITH ME

❦

Walking with Me means practicing My presence in each of your daily affairs, each twenty-four hours I've given you.

- It means asking Me for the strength to face each day.
- It means turning to Me and asking prayer for yourself and others.
- It means thanking Me for the blessings you have received during the day.

Believe that I am beside you in Spirit to help you and guide you along the way each day.

I won't ever leave you or forsake you. I am walking with you.

❦

"The LORD will guide you always; he will satisfy your needs in a sun-scorched land and will strengthen your frame. You will be like a well-watered garden, like a spring whose waters never fail." —Isaiah 58:11

❦

PRAYER:

Thank you, Lord, for walking with me. I don't have
enough words to express my gratitude; however, You
see my heart and know how grateful I am.
I am so appreciative of Your faithfulness to me.
I love you so!

REFLECTION:

WAY OF LIFE

⊂⊃⊂⊃

This life of faith is a way of life.

I'm teaching you how to live this life, because you have to learn it if you want to live with peace and joy.

I will point you in the direction you need to go, twenty-four hours at a time. Start your twenty-four hours each day with Me.

You are learning mental and emotional balance and how to ask that My Will be done in every situation. This helps you to relax and not get tense with fear. This balance, which comes with peace, will be noticed by others, people who crave it, in this vacillating, unstable world.

You can claim My power in any situation and be able to use it.

Always come back to Me to replenish your strength.

⊂⊃⊂⊃

"For the kingdom of God is not a matter of eating and drinking, but of righteousness, peace and joy in the Holy Spirit . . ."
—Romans 14:17

⊂⊃⊂⊃

PRAYER:

I love you, Lord, for teaching me the way of life. Thank you for caring for me by counseling me on what is important. I'm so thankful I never have to live without You!

I love you!

REFLECTION:

WEAKNESS

CXEXO

Your weakness attracts Me because My power and strength are available for you.

Don't belittle yourself when you feel weak, and don't fear weakness.

Call on My strength and it will be there for you.

Your weakness can be your greatest strength. Face it. You know what it is. Use it to go forward. Set this weakness in the center of your mind. Examine it and trace it to its original origin. See why it is a weakness. Use it as a strength—because when you honestly face a weakness and set it in the center of your awareness, it starts becoming a strength.

If you find another weakness, handle it the same way, one weakness at a time.

Trust Me enough and your weakness won't matter.

CXEXO

"But God chose the foolish things of the world to shame the wise; God chose the weak things of the world to shame the strong."
—1 Corinthians 1:27

"But he said to me, "My grace is sufficient for you, for my power is made perfect in weakness." Therefore I will boast all the more gladly about my weaknesses, so that Christ's power may rest on me. 10 That is why, for Christ's sake, I delight in weaknesses, in insults, in hardships, in persecutions, in difficulties. For when I am weak, then I am strong." —2 Corinthians 2:9-10

REFLECTION:

WEARINESS

࿊

The world's cares and distractions at times can wear you down. Don't yield to this because your spirit will become weak.

My Spirit is always with you to build you back up, replenish you, and renew you.

Seek My help.

When you are overcome by temporary conditions beyond your control, make a time of rest and spend quiet communion with Me. Keep quiet and wait for Me to revive and restore.

I love you.

࿊

"And the God of all grace, who called you to his eternal glory in Christ, after you have suffered a little while, will himself restore you and make you strong, firm and steadfast."
—1 Peter 5:10

REFLECTION:

WISDOM

༺⬥༻

I am the true source of wisdom and knowledge.
Faith in Me is the only road to salvation and the only answer
to the secrets of life.

Wisdom is being able to see the long view of consequences before making choices. No matter how good something looks, look at the long view. When you accept a behavior into your life, you are accepting the end result of that behavior.

༺⬥༻

"The fear of the LORD is the beginning of wisdom; all who follow his precepts have good understanding. To him belongs eternal praise." —Psalm 111:10

"For the LORD gives wisdom; from his mouth come knowledge and understanding." —Proverbs 2:6

REFLECTION:

WORK

ᘓ୫୦

Do your work as unto Me.
Do it as a love offering to Me.
Do it heartily from your soul because you love Me.
I will be with you. I see you. I'm pleased with you.

Discard thoughts of trying to please people. Do work to your very best for Me. I have called you to this work and I am faithful to you. I am totally trustworthy and I will fulfill this call.

Trust Me. Depend on Me.

Draw on My strength, My wisdom, My sharpness, and My mental clarity. I will do it.

Your real life's work is to grow spiritually. To do this, diligently seek Me and My Will for your life. As you do this, you will continue to reach greater spiritual heights.

ᘓ୫୦

"And whatever you do, whether in word or deed, do it all in the name of the Lord Jesus, giving thanks to God the Father through him. . . . Whatever you do, work at it with all your heart, as working for the Lord, not for human masters . . ." —Colossians 3:17, 23

"The one who calls you is faithful, and he will do it." — 1 Thessalonians 5:24

REFLECTION:

WORRY

When you worry, you are focusing on the problem instead of focusing on Me.
Give Me your problems, one by one, and pray, "Thy Will be done." Let go of each one and watch Me work. You will be amazed at what I can do when you get out of the way.
Worry is terrible mental punishment. Don't worry about the future or anything else.

When you allow yourself to be upset and worried over one thing,
you succeed only in opening the door for hundreds of other things.

Don't worry about tomorrow. You have no idea what tomorrow will bring, but I do. I will take care of you. Faith is not seeing but believing. Choose faith. Your life is changing from defeat to victory.

Stay sheltered in My love, grace, and mercy. I will relieve you of the weight of worry, depression, misery, and heartache if you will let me.

Lift up your eyes and see Me in the universe and in others.

"Whoever dwells in the shelter of the Most High will rest in the shadow of the Almighty." —Psalm 91:1

REFLECTION:

WORRY II

CREASE

Life is getting yourself and your mind under control.
Can you remember what you were worrying about two
weeks ago? You will probably find it difficult to remember.
Then why should you worry over problems that arise today?

Change your attitude toward them by putting them in My
hands. Trust Me. My Will for you is the best and I will work
everything out for your good and for My glory.

When you let Me relieve you of the burden of your problems, then you can face them without fear.

CREASE

*"Humble yourselves, therefore, under God's
mighty hand, that he may lift you up in due
time. Cast all your anxiety on him because he
cares for you."* — 1 Peter 5:6-7

REFLECTION:

WORRY III

☙❦❧

Don't bring into today what you might do tomorrow.
Worry causes fear. You cannot have worry and peace at the same time.
Don't let your life be ruined by worry and fear.
Give Me the situation and pray, "Thy Will be done."

☙❦❧

"Be anxious for nothing, but in everything by prayer and supplication, with thanksgiving, let your requests be made known to God; and the peace of God, which surpasses all understanding, will guard your hearts and minds through Christ Jesus." —Philippians 4:6-7 NKJV

REFLECTION:

WORSHIP

⌘

When you look at this universe and realize there is more than what you will ever know or experience, you are worshiping.

I am the Creator of everything—from the beginning to the end. You will never know how big this is.

I created order and laws, and I rule over all.
When you feel awe, you are worshiping.
When you feel appreciation, you are worshiping.
When you feel wonder and amazement, you are worshiping.
Beyond your space and time, the universe is eternal and limitless.
My power is behind it all.

You can experience My power in you. Worship Me by offering yourself as a living sacrifice. Ask Me to help you devote your mind, heart, and body to becoming who I want you to be. Honor Me with your life.

⌘

"Therefore, I urge you . . . in view of God's mercy, to offer your bodies as living sacrifices,

holy and pleasing to God—this is your spiritual act of worship."—Romans 12:1

"When I consider your heavens, the work of your fingers, the moon and the stars, which you have set in place, what is man that you are mindful of him, the son of man that you care for him?"—Psalm 8:3-4

REFLECTION:

YOUR MIND

CR8O

Your mind is wandering less and less.

The fantasizing and daydreaming are fading away and you are living in reality more and more.

You are setting your mind on Me and things above and not so much on things of the earth. Your mind is becoming more and more stable and peaceful.

You are seeing beauty, goodness, and purpose in the world. You are seeing Me.

Remember that faith doesn't deny reality.

You will be renewed. You will be remade, but you need My help. As My Spirit flows through you, I will sweep away the past hurts.

Your mind has to be reeducated to be grateful daily and to enjoy living a simple, healthy, normal life.

Your outlook is changing.

CR8O

". . . . The mind controlled by the Spirit is life and peace." —Romans 8:6

"Since, then, you have been raised with Christ, set your hearts on things above, where Christ is seated at the right hand of God." —Colossians 3:1

"Do not conform any longer to the pattern of this world, but be transformed by the renewing of your mind. Then you will be able to test and approve what God's will is—his good, pleasing and perfect will." —Romans 12:2

REFLECTION:

"I Love You"—
God's Promise to You

⁜

Have you always wanted someone who would never leave you?
"I" am here.
I will never leave you or forsake you.
"Indeed, the very hairs of your head are all numbered."—Luke 12:7

⁜

Have you always wanted someone who would understand you?
"I" am here.
"You know when I sit and when I rise; you perceive my thoughts from afar."
—Psalm 139:2

⁜

Have you always wanted someone who would intimately love you?
"I" am here.

"... neither height nor depth, nor anything else in all creation, will be able to separate us from the love of God that is in Christ Jesus our Lord."—Romans 8:39

෮෫෨

Have you always wanted to be someone's "center of attention"?

"I" am here.

"See, I have engraved you on the palms of my hands; your walls are ever before me."
—Isaiah 49:16

෮෫෨

You are worth the price of My only Son.

෮෫෨

"But God shows and clearly proves His [own] love for us by the fact that while we were still sinners, Christ (the Messiah, the Anointed One) died for us. Therefore, since we are now justified (acquitted, made righteous, and brought into right relationship with God) by Christ's blood, how much more [certain is it that] we shall be saved by Him

from the indignation and wrath of God." —
Romans 5:8-9 AMP

ᙧᘓᘔ

I chose you. You didn't choose Me.

ᙧᘓᘔ

"You have not chosen Me, but I have chosen you and I have appointed you [I have planted you], that you might go and bear fruit and keep on bearing, and that your fruit may be lasting [that it may remain, abide], so that whatever you ask the Father in My Name [as presenting all that I Am], He may give it to you." —John 15:16 AMP

REFLECTION:

ABOUT THE AUTHOR

Patti Miller Dunham
Pattimillerdunham.com, pattimillerdunham@me.com

CRWD

Family is a big part of Patti Miller Dunham's life. Sixty-nine years old, she has taken care of her ninety-five-year-old mother for nine years. Also close by live her daughter, son-in-law, and two grandsons who claim their Grammy is "their biggest fan." Recently, she has married the love of her life (her high school sweetheart), and has received the bonus of two fantastic stepsons, two beautiful daughters-in-law, and four more phenomenal grandchildren.

Even though everyone would describe Dunham as a caregiver, always putting family first, she found the time for success in many realms of the business world. Her business success started in the cosmetics industry where she launched a successful South Texas territory for a national cosmetics company. Later she founded her own cosmetics company and watched it grow throughout thirty states across the United States. With the business entrepreneur spirit growing inside her, she moved on and co-founded an international photography supply company, which has stayed in the family for twenty-two years.

Since 1978, Dunham has conducted an adjunct-speaking career. As a speaker at major conventions across the United States and Hawaii, Patti was asked by the Zig Ziglar Corporation if it could reproduce one of her speeches to train their own salespeople. Her life testimony of how she found Jesus Christ through the challenges that she faced then put her on the speaking circuit for Stonecroft Ministries and other Christian events across the United States. Her growing desire to help others and share what she learned from her walk with Jesus in her circle of life led her to write inspirational columns, and she has published articles in many different periodicals.

Dunham published her first popular book in 2010. *"I Saw Heaven!"* is an inspirational story about life-changing conversations that she had with her brother after his near death experience.

Her second book, *Living Right Side Up in an Upside Down World*, is a sequel to *"I Saw Heaven!,"* and it continues her intimate, personal conversations with God.

Both books are available as an eBook, in any Christian bookstore, or online.

If you would like to contact Patti or request a speaking engagement for your group, please contact her at pattimillerdunham@me.com or through her Website at http://www.pattimillerdunham.com.

She would be delighted to hear from you.